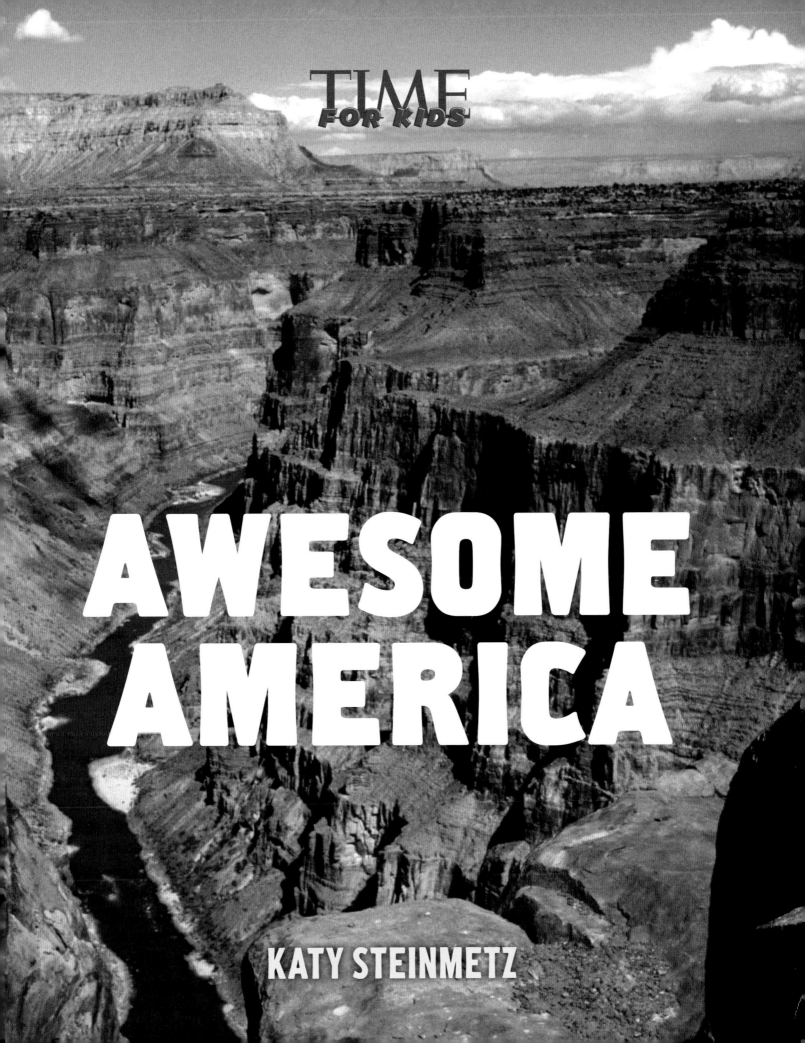

AWESOME AMERICA

KATY STEINMETZ

TIME FOR KIDS

TIME FOR KIDS EDITOR: Brenda Iasevoli
TIME INC. BOOKS EDITOR: Deirdre Langeland
ART DIRECTOR: Georgia Morrissey
PHOTO RESEARCHER: Nataki Hewling
DESIGNER: Mike Leister
PRODUCTION MANAGER: Hillary Leary
ASSOCIATE PREPRESS MANAGER: Alex Voznesenskiy

Published by Liberty Street, an imprint of Time Inc. Books
225 Liberty Street
New York, New York 10281

LIBERTY STREET is a trademark of Time Inc.

ISBN 10: 1-61893-149-0
ISBN 13: 978-1-61893-149-8
Library of Congress Control Number: 2016935478
First edition, 2016
1 QGV 16

10 9 8 7 6 5 4 3 2 1

Time Inc. Books products may be purchased for business or promotional use. For
information on bulk purchases, please contact Christi Crowley in the Special Sales
Department at (845) 895-9858.

To order Time Inc. Books Collector's Editions, please call (800) 327-6388, Monday
through Friday, 7 a.m.-9 p.m., Central Time.

We welcome your comments and suggestions about Time Inc. Books.
Please write to us at:
Time Inc. Books
Attention: Book Editors
P.O. Box 62310
Tampa, Florida 33662-2310
timeincbooks.com

TABLE OF CONTENTS

CHAPTER 1: Our Beginning 4

FIND OUT: Who was first to call America home?
LEARN: How America got started
TAKE A CLOSER LOOK: Clothes our Founding Fathers wore

CHAPTER 2: Our Government 20

FIND OUT: What's in the U.S. Constitution?
LEARN: How the three branches of government work
TAKE A CLOSER LOOK: Symbols in the presidential seal

CHAPTER 3: Our Presidents 38

FIND OUT: Who can be president of the United States?
LEARN: Fun facts about the White House's famous residents
TAKE A CLOSER LOOK: The president's private jet

CHAPTER 4: Tour the Fifty States 50

FIND OUT: What is each state's claim to fame?
LEARN: The nickname of every state
TAKE A CLOSER LOOK: America's capital city, Washington, D.C.

CHAPTER 5: The Land 64

FIND OUT: Where are America's highest, lowest, and hottest places?
LEARN: Fascinating facts about America's natural landmarks
TAKE A CLOSER LOOK: Wild animals that call America home

CHAPTER 6: Coming to America 78

FIND OUT: Why did millions risk their lives to come to America?
LEARN: The accomplishments of notable immigrants
TAKE A CLOSER LOOK: Statue of Liberty

CHAPTER 7: Moments That Changed America 92

FIND OUT: What are the events that shaped America?
LEARN: Who took the first steps on the moon
TAKE A CLOSER LOOK: Ford's Model T

CHAPTER 8: Civil Rights 106

FIND OUT: How did the struggle for equal rights develop in America?
LEARN: The history of the civil rights movement
TAKE A CLOSER LOOK: American Indians take over Alcatraz

CHAPTER 9: Great Americans 120

FIND OUT: Who are the most influential Americans?
LEARN: How some Americans have done our country proud
TAKE A CLOSER LOOK: Walt Disney movies

CHAPTER 10: Growing Up in America 136

FIND OUT: Could you live to be 140 years old?
LEARN: What makes Americans happy
TAKE A CLOSER LOOK: Life in America through the centuries

CHAPTER 11: America's Role in the World 148

FIND OUT: How has America made its mark around the world?
LEARN: Where emoji came from
TAKE A CLOSER LOOK: Great U.S. athletes

CHAPTER 12: America's Home-Grown Gifts to the World 162

FIND OUT: What are America's greatest innovations?
LEARN: The origins of American music
TAKE A CLOSER LOOK: American inventions

CHAPTER 13: One of a Kind 176

FIND OUT: Who is on the $100,000 bill?
LEARN: How to talk like an American
TAKE A CLOSER LOOK: Top U.S. tourist spots

CHAPTER 14: Year by Year 190

TAKE A CLOSER LOOK: Events that shaped America over the past 400 years

Glossary 202

Explore Some More 204

Credits 206

Index 208

Chapter 1

OUR BEGINNING

The Founding Fathers present the first draft of the Declaration of Independence to the Second Continental Congress. Less than a week later, on July 4, 1776, the delegates signed the document, declaring the American colonies' freedom from Britain. Read on to learn more about the birth of our country. Standing at the left side of the table, left to right, are: John Adams, Roger Sherman, Robert Livingston, Thomas Jefferson, and Benjamin Franklin. John Hancock is seated.

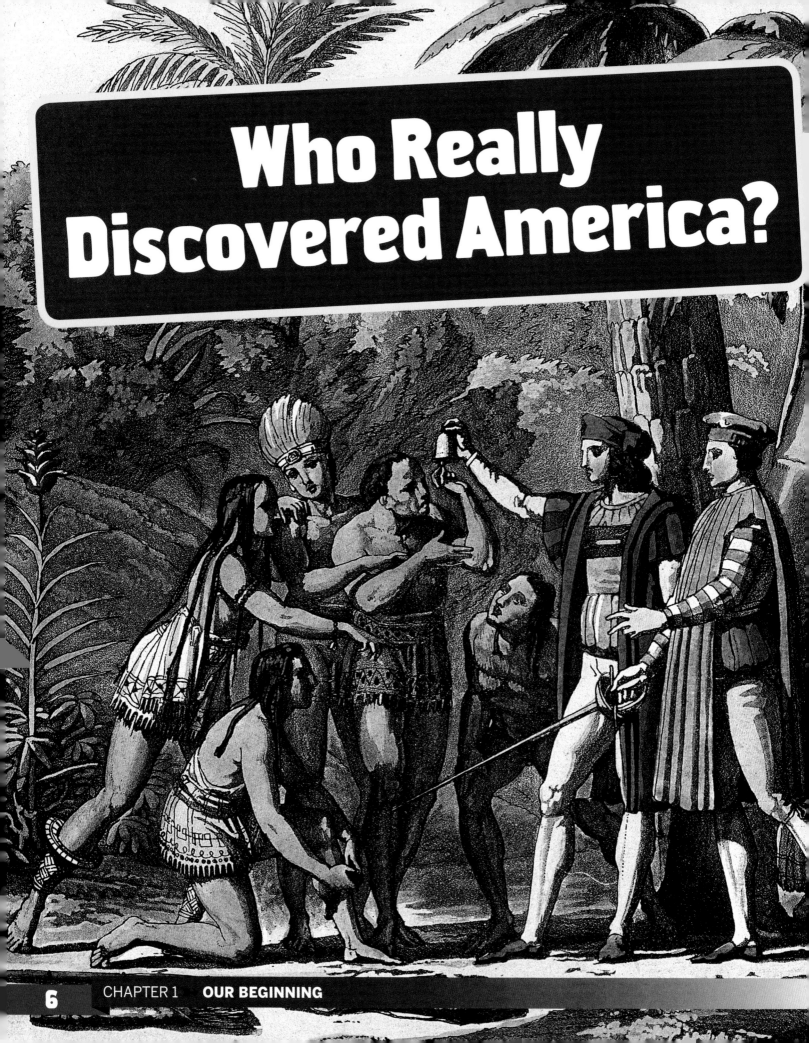

Who Really Discovered America?

For many years, Americans have celebrated Columbus as a hero, which is why a day in October was declared Columbus Day. But the explorer enslaved native people he encountered on his trips. Today, some celebrate Indigenous Peoples' Day in October instead, to honor native people who were here before the Europeans.

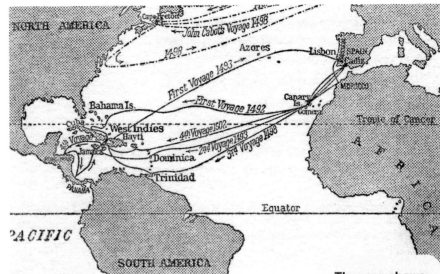

The map shows the route Columbus took from Spain to the New World.

Many children (including kids who may now be your parents) were taught that an Italian named Christopher Columbus discovered America. It's true that more than 500 years ago the explorer sailed to America from Spain. He and his crew landed in what Europeans called the "New World" on October 12, 1492. But he wasn't the first to step foot on this land.

Historians believe that native people lived here more than 10,000 years ago. At least one other explorer beat Columbus to the punch, too. Many historians believe Viking Leif Erikson crossed the Atlantic Ocean from Europe and landed his boat on the American shore nearly 300 years before Columbus did! Other explorers, from lands as far away as Asia and the Middle East, may also have been here before 1492.

Still, Columbus has an important place in history. His voyages uncovered a continent that most Europeans didn't know existed, kicking off hundreds of years of exploration in what would later be known as America.

Though there's no evidence that Viking warriors actually wore horned helmets, those Northern Europeans are shown wearing these intimidating hats in movies and paintings.

The Really, Really Early Settlers

Long before the fifty states existed, native people lived on the land that is now America. Historians believe that their ancestors crossed a "land bridge" that connected Asia to North America during the last ice age. (See map: right.) For thousands of years before Europeans arrived, these people lived in their own societies with their own governments.

Native people in the U.S. are

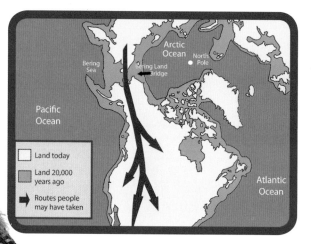

The map shows the routes early tribes took across a land bridge that once linked Russia to Alaska.

Arctic Ocean
North Pole
Bering Sea
Bering Land Bridge
Pacific Ocean
Atlantic Ocean

Land today
Land 20,000 years ago
Routes people may have taken

called American Indians. But it is best to refer to each tribal group by its name. There are hundreds of different groups of American Indians, such as the Chippewa, Navajo, Cherokee, and Sioux.

You have probably seen the feather headdresses and the homes some Indian tribes built of buffalo skins and wooden poles, called tepees. What you may not know is that today, there are 567 Indian tribes recognized by the government. Many tribe members live on lands inside the U.S. where they can govern themselves. They were forced to move away from their homes so that the newly-founded nation could grow. (You can read more about this in Chapter 8.)

Left: A Native Alaskan mother in 1916. Her ancestors would have crossed the land bridge thousands of years earlier. Top: A North American headdress

This 1871 wood engraving shows Pacific Northwest Indians fishing in the Columbia River in Washington Territory.

A medicine man from the Sioux tribe stands in front of a tepee on the Great Plains.

Some American Indians used stone tomahawks as tools and weapons.

There are only about 5 million American Indians in the U.S. today, about 1.5% of the population, but the words they have used are everywhere. You've probably used a bunch without even knowing it! About half the states in the U.S. got their names from Indian languages. Missouri, named after the Missouri Indian tribe, means "wooden canoe people." The names for many animals—like raccoon, moose, and skunk—also come from Indian words.

The Hardy Boys and Girls Who Started America

America now has thousands of cities, from giant metropolitan areas full of skyscrapers in New York to tiny towns full of surfers in Hawaii. But there is a first for everything. And the first successful colony settled by the British was a little place called Jamestown, in present-day Virginia. About 214 men and boys built a home there in 1607.

The group that started Jamestown had a hard life. First they had to make a five-month-long trip across 3,000 miles of dangerous seas. When they arrived in America, the land was a wild, unknown place. They had trouble finding food. Many of the settlers got sick and starved. Some got so hungry that they ate the leather on their belts.

Indian tribes helped the settlers by giving them food, sometimes in exchange for metal tools. But the settlers and Indians also warred, leading to conflict that lasted centuries. With the arrival of more settlers, especially women needed for starting families, the colony survived.

The settlers who came to Jamestown were hoping to find silver and gold. But many other early Americans, like the Pilgrims who landed in Massachusetts in 1620, came to America in search of freedom. In parts of Europe people were once expected to follow a specific religion. Those who didn't were persecuted. So brave travelers left their homelands to find a place where they could worship freely.

In 1620, a three-masted ship called the *Mayflower* brought Pilgrims from England to America.

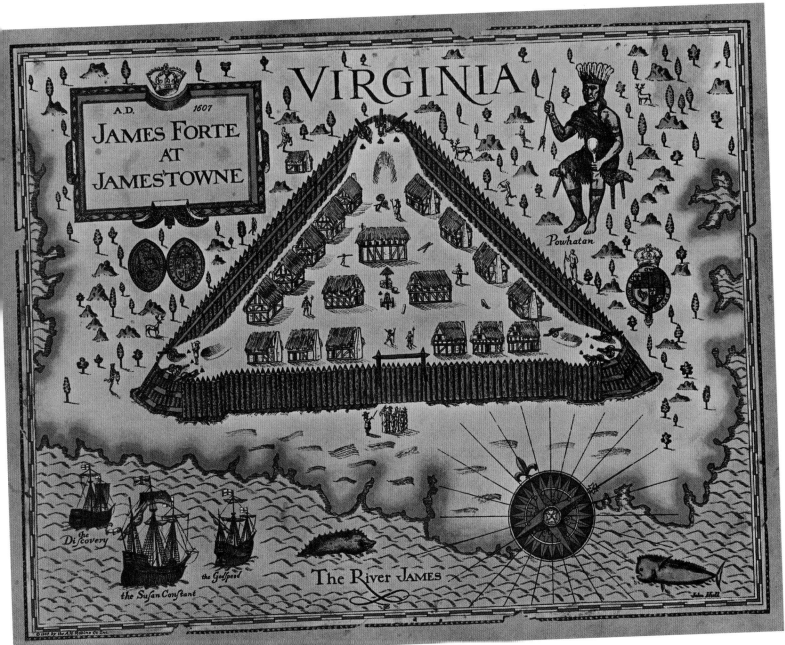

VIRGINIA

A.D. 1607

JAMES FORTE
AT
JAMESTOWNE

Powhatan

the Discovery

the Godspeed

the Susan Constant

The River JAMES

This 1607 plan of Jamestown, Virginia, shows the settlement's triangle-shaped fort.

The Pilgrims traveled to America on the *Mayflower* in 1620. William Bradford summed up the risky journey like this: "All great and honorable actions are accompanied with great difficulties, and both must be enterprised and overcome with answerable courage." President John F. Kennedy quoted those words when he argued that American astronauts needed to travel to the moon, which they later did in "one giant leap for mankind" in 1969.

Meet the Founding Fathers

About   **Profiles**   **Events**   **Photos**

Eventually America grew to be 13 colonies, all ruled by Britain. As it did, some babies were born who would one day change the course of history. As these babies grew into boys, America grew restless and unhappy with British rule. When these boys grew into men, they led the Revolutionary War to fight for freedom from the British. Their efforts made America its own independent country. These historic giants became known as the Founding Fathers.

George Washington
FIRST PRESIDENT OF THE UNITED STATES

Past Commander-in-chief of the Continental Army, farmer, country gentleman

⚑ **Life Events**

- 1732 Born in Virginia on a farm, where he mastered tobacco growing
- 1752 Inherited Mount Vernon estate, where he farmed and raised animals
- 1753 Started military career
- 1759 Married Martha Dandridge Custis, who would one day become the first first lady of the U.S.
- 1774 Participated in the First Continental Congress, a meeting where colonies discussed how to respond to "intolerable acts" by the British
- 1775 Appointed commander-in-chief of the Continental Army
- 1781 Won victory at Yorktown, Virginia, the last major battle of the Revolution
- 1789 Elected first president of the United States
- 1799 Died, after a lifetime of accomplishments and problems with his teeth

John Adams
SECOND PRESIDENT OF THE UNITED STATES

Past Diplomat to Britain and France, author, teacher, lawyer

⚑ **Life Events**

- 1735 Born in Braintree, Massachusetts
- 1751 Admitted to Harvard College at age 15
- 1755 Started keeping a diary he would continue writing all his life
- 1758 Became a lawyer
- 1764 Married Abigail Smith, who became an advocate for women's rights
- 1767 Fathered John Quincy, who would become the sixth U.S. president
- 1776 Outlined a new American government with three branches
- 1783 Negotiated peace treaty with Britain to end the war
- 1789 Elected the country's first vice president
- 1796 Elected second president of the United States
- 1798 Established the Department of the Navy
- 1826 Died on July 4, the same day as Thomas Jefferson

Thomas Jefferson
THIRD PRESIDENT OF THE UNITED STATES

Past Founder of the University of Virginia, philosopher, lawyer

▷ **Life Events**

- 1743 Born in Virginia
- 1760 Entered College of William and Mary, spending 15 hours a day reading and three practicing the violin
- 1762 Started studying to become a lawyer
- 1776 Wrote the Declaration of Independence
- 1779 Started serving as governor of Virginia
- 1790 Appointed first secretary of state, who represents Americans abroad
- 1797 Served as vice president of the United States
- 1801 Served as third president of the United States
- 1809 Retired from elected office
- 1819 Founded the University of Virginia
- 1826 Died on July 4, the same day as John Adams

James Madison
FOURTH PRESIDENT OF THE UNITED STATES

Past "Father of the Constitution," Congressman, secretary of state

▷ **Life Events**

- 1751 Born in Port Conway, Virginia, the first of 12 children
- 1769 Enrolled in Princeton University and finished college in two years
- 1780 Elected to the Continental Congress, the body that governed the colonies during the Revolutionary War
- 1788 Helped write the Federalist Papers, essays encouraging states to vote in favor of the Constitution
- 1789 Elected to the U.S. House of Representatives and proposed the first ten amendments to the Constitution
- 1808 Elected America's fourth president
- 1836 Died after years of running his family farm in Virginia

Alexander Hamilton
FIRST SECRETARY OF THE TREASURY

Past Army officer, lawyer, clerk, founded the *New York Post*

▷ **Life Events**

- 1755 Born in the British West Indies (islands in the Caribbean)
- 1766 Worked as a clerk, starting at the age of 11
- 1774 Attended King's College in New York
- 1776 Became an Army captain in the Revolutionary War and befriended George Washington
- 1778 In a dangerous battle (and close call!), had his horse shot out from under him
- 1782 Became a lawyer and was elected to the Congress of the Confederation
- 1788 Helped write the Federalist Papers, arguing for states to vote in favor of the Constitution and strong national government
- 1789 Became the first secretary of the Treasury, the person in charge of the country's money
- 1804 Accepted a challenge to a duel with then-vice president Aaron Burr and was killed

Benjamin Franklin
INVENTOR, AUTHOR, DIPLOMAT

Past First postmaster general (head of the U.S. Post Office)

▷ **Life Events**

- 1706 Born in Boston
- 1716 Left school at age 10 to work at his father's candle shop
- 1722 Became a vegetarian (partly so he could spend more money on books)
- 1729 Bought the *Pennsylvania Gazette*
- 1752 Conducted kite experiment that led to understanding electricity
- 1776 Sent to France as a diplomat to secure help in the Revolutionary War
- 1783 Negotiated peace with Britain
- 1784 Invented bifocal glasses, allowing for viewing of things near and far
- 1890 Died in Philadelphia at age 84

Why Were Americans Ready to Revolt?

Britain ruled the colonies in America from thousands of miles away. Britain also demanded that the Americans pay taxes on items like stamps, sugar, and tea. Some taxes are necessary—it costs money to run a country and colonies—but Americans felt the taxes were too harsh.

To make matters worse, Britain wouldn't allow America to send a representative to cast votes in Parliament, where British lawmakers were deciding how to rule the colonies. This led to the complaint that there was "taxation without representation." Some of the Founding Fathers argued that America needed to be free of the British once and for all, and people started listening.

Not all parties are filled with cake and balloons. When the British started taxing tea, the colonists decided to do something about it. Groups of men disguised as "American Indians" boarded three ships in Boston and threw 342 chests of tea into the water in 1773. The Americans' act of defiance became known as the Boston Tea Party.

CRAVAT

Men almost always wore some kind of cloth around their necks. A cravat was one type of necktie, typically made of linen and lace.

WIG

Men once found it fashionable to wear wigs made from human hair. Some wigs were made from the hair of goats and other animals.

IT'S HOW THEY WORE IT

On the night of the Boston Tea Party, the colonial men wore costumes. But even the clothes they wore every day might seem like costumes to us.

SHIRT

Ruffles adorned the necks and wrists of some men's shirts.

COAT/ WAISTCOAT

On their top, men wore tight-fitting vests called waistcoats. These could be made from cotton, silk, linen, or wool.

BREECHES

Men covered their bottom halves with breeches that fell just below the knees and were fastened by buttons.

COAT

Men wore long-sleeved, heavy coats. Some reached well past the knees.

LEGGINGS

These stockings kept men's calves warm.

SHOES

Men's shoes were usually black with heels and buckles.

The Shot Heard 'Round the World

This engraving depicts Paul Revere as he rides to warn of British soldiers marching toward Concord, Massachusetts, on April 18, 1775.

Americans weighed carefully the decision to go to war with Britain. Lives were at stake. Britain was a powerful country. But as more and more Americans grew unhappy, people started collecting weapons. They stored cannonballs and gunpowder in a little Massachusetts town called Concord, about 20 miles from Boston.

When the British discovered in 1775 that Americans were stockpiling weapons—which was against the law—they decided to take action. British soldiers, called Redcoats, planned to snatch the weapons from the colonists.

Paul Revere learned of the plan. He sent a spy to the British camp to find out how the British would arrive. The spy was to flash a

The Americans who met the British in Lexington that day called themselves minutemen, for their ability to be ready to fight at a moment's notice.

lantern once if the British planned to go by land, twice if by sea.

On the night of April 18, 1775, the lantern flashed twice. Paul Revere and a man named William Dawes took off on their horses to warn fellow colonists.

The colonists met the British at a town called Lexington. The 70 or so American volunteers were about to fight more than 200 professional British soldiers. No one knows who fired first, but we do know that, despite the odds against them, and after a long day of fighting on April 19, the Americans were not defeated. And the war began.

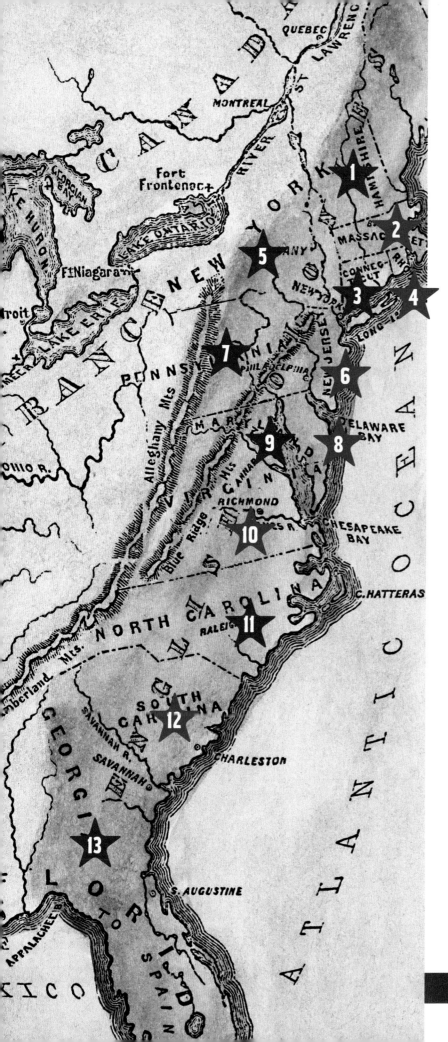

A NEW NATION IS BORN

The war started in 1775 and lasted eight years, ending with America winning its independence from Britain. In 1776, the Founding Fathers named the new country the United States of America. By 1790, all 13 colonies had entered the Union and become the nation's first 13 states.

1 NEW HAMPSHIRE
ESTABLISHED AS A COLONY: 1623
STATEHOOD: 1788

2 MASSACHUSETTS
ESTABLISHED AS A COLONY: 1620
STATEHOOD: 1788

3 CONNECTICUT
ESTABLISHED AS A COLONY: 1636
STATEHOOD: 1788

4 RHODE ISLAND
ESTABLISHED AS A COLONY: 1636
STATEHOOD: 1790

5 NEW YORK
ESTABLISHED AS A COLONY: 1664
STATEHOOD: 1788

6 NEW JERSEY
ESTABLISHED AS A COLONY: 1664
STATEHOOD: 1787

7 PENNSYLVANIA
ESTABLISHED AS A COLONY: 1681
STATEHOOD: 1787

8 DELAWARE
ESTABLISHED AS A COLONY: 1664
STATEHOOD: 1787

9 MARYLAND
ESTABLISHED AS A COLONY: 1632
STATEHOOD: 1788

10 VIRGINIA
ESTABLISHED AS A COLONY: 1607
STATEHOOD: 1788

11 NORTH CAROLINA
ESTABLISHED AS A COLONY: 1663
STATEHOOD: 1789

12 SOUTH CAROLINA
ESTABLISHED AS A COLONY: 1663
STATEHOOD: 1788

13 GEORGIA
ESTABLISHED AS A COLONY: 1732
STATEHOOD: 1788

Really Important Pieces of Paper

W ords have shaped the fates of countries, and the lives of millions. Documents, and people's belief in them, made the United States what it is today. Here are some of the greats.

THE MAYFLOWER COMPACT

WRITTEN IN: 1620
SIGNED BY: Early English colonists settling in America
WRITTEN BECAUSE: New settlers who arrived at Plymouth, Massachusetts, including the Pilgrims, needed a document to keep peace among themselves. The Mayflower Compact was a promise by all to follow laws for the good of everyone. Named for the ship they traveled on, this short document was the first one to spell out ideas that make the American government work.
GREAT LINE: "We…combine ourselves into a civil Body Politik, for our better ordering and preservation."

MAGNA CARTA

Magna Carta of King John, AD 1215

WRITTEN IN: 1215
SIGNED BY: Powerful Englishmen known as barons and England's King John
WRITTEN BECAUSE: This piece of paper made peace between the barons and King John, who were warring. It was a constitution, a document that explains how a country will be governed. The Founding Fathers looked to the Magna Carta for ideas when declaring their liberty from Britain.
GREAT LINE: "To no one will we deny or delay right or justice."

COMMON SENSE

COMMON SENSE;
ADDRESSED TO THE
INHABITANTS
OF
AMERICA,
On the following interesting
SUBJECTS.

I. Of the Origin and Design of Government in general, with concise Remarks on the English Constitution.
II. Of Monarchy and Hereditary Succession.
III. Thoughts on the present State of American Affairs.
IV. Of the present Ability of America, with some miscellaneous Reflections.

Man knows no Master save creating HEAVEN,
Or those whom choice and common good ordain.
THOMSON.

PHILADELPHIA;
Printed, and Sold, by R. BELL, in Third-Street.
MDCCLXXVI.

WRITTEN IN: January 1776
WRITTEN BY: A Founding Father named Thomas Paine
WRITTEN BECAUSE: Paine wrote this document arguing for Americans to declare their independence from Britain at a time when some colonists wanted independence and others didn't. It united people and politicians behind a single idea, and prepared them to face powerful Britain together.
GREAT LINE: "From the errors of other nations, let us learn wisdom."

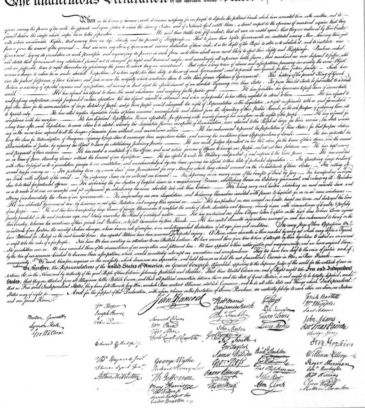

DECLARATION OF INDEPENDENCE

WRITTEN IN: **July 1776**

WRITTEN BY: **Thomas Jefferson and other Founding Fathers**

WRITTEN BECAUSE: **This document formally declared that the American colonies would no longer be run by Britain. Instead, they would be their own country, the United States of America. This document explains why America was tired of British rule and wanted to be free. When the Founding Fathers signed it, the war was officially on.**

GREAT LINE: **"We hold these truths to be self-evident; that all men are created equal."**

> ## " We hold these truths to be self-evident; that all men are created equal. "

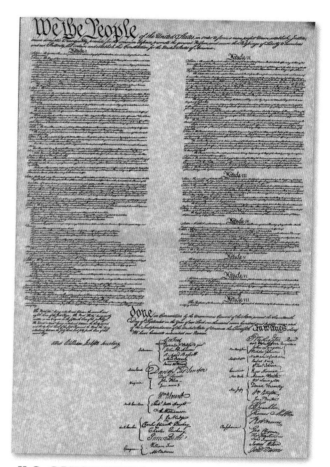

U.S. CONSTITUTION

WRITTEN IN: **1787**

WRITTEN BY: **The Founding Fathers**

WRITTEN BECAUSE: **After Americans won independence, they still had a big job ahead of them: setting up a whole country. The Constitution outlined America's government and promised citizens basic rights. Today, this document remains the highest law in the land.**

GREAT LINE: **"We the People of the United States, in order to form a more perfect Union...do ordain and establish this Constitution for the United States of America."**

TREATY OF PARIS

WRITTEN IN: **1783**

SIGNED BY: **Leaders from America and Britain**

WRITTEN BECAUSE: **This document was a peace treaty that ended the war between America and Britain. The treaty made America an independent country. The document set American borders, the boundaries of the country. Britain also promised to give America lands. The treaty was signed in Paris. That's how it got its name.**

GREAT LINE: **"His Brittanic Majesty acknowledges the said United States...to be free sovereign and independent states."**

Chapter 2

OUR GOVERNMENT

IN GOD WE TRUST

The president, Congress, and the Supreme Court operate the U.S. government. Here the president and Congress are at work. Each of their jobs is defined in the Constitution. Read on to learn how this document keeps our country running.

The U.S. Constitution

On September 17, 1787, 39 men signed one of history's most important documents: the U.S. Constitution. It contains 4,543 words that define how our government works and protect basic rights of citizens. More than 200 years later, the U.S. Constitution remains the law of the land.

After the American Revolution, the states operated more like friends than family. Each state was independent. To make the country stronger and more unified, representatives from each state met in 1787. For a whole summer, the men debated how to join the states under a single set of rules. Their compromises became the Constitution.

The framers of the Constitution wanted a balanced government. They wanted the United States to be strong. But they didn't want government leaders to become so strong that they could do whatever they wanted, even if their actions made the people unhappy. The colonies had just fought a war to end that kind of tyranny!

The year was 1787. The place: Philadelphia's State House. Our Founding Fathers, depicted in this painting, established the rules of our government in the U.S. Constitution.

WHAT IS A CITIZEN?

cit·i·zen *[sidizən, sidisən]*

A citizen is a legal resident of a country who has the rights and protection of that country.

The Constitution is four pages long, and each page is about 29 inches by 24 inches. That's a little smaller than a stop sign. Americans can see the Constitution in Washington, D.C., where it's displayed in the most advanced picture frames in the world. The frames protect the fragile artifact from people's fingers, changing temperatures, and old age. The cases that hold the Constitution, the Bill of Rights, and the Declaration of Independence cost more than $5 million!

Three is Better Than One

James Madison, the fourth U.S. president, is known as the "Father of the Constitution." In 1787, at the Constitutional Convention in Philadelphia, Pennsylvania, he helped outline a plan for a strong national government with three branches. The branches have different duties that allow them to keep an eye on one another. This system of checks and balances ensures that no one branch has greater power over the others.

THREE BRANCHE

1. LEGISLATIVE BRANCH: LAWMAKERS
Congress
100 Senators and 435 Representatives
Duties include:
• Writing bills, then voting on whether the bills should become law
• Collecting money from taxes
• Declaring war

2

3

OF THE UNITED STATES GOVERNMENT

2. EXECUTIVE BRANCH: LAW ENFORCERS

The president, vice president, and Cabinet members

Duties include:

• Signing bills into law or vetoing laws

• Appointing Supreme Court justices

• Meeting with foreign leaders and negotiating treaties

3. JUDICIAL BRANCH: LAW REFEREES

Nine Supreme Court justices

Duties include:

• Deciding if laws agree with the Constitution

• Interpreting how laws should be applied

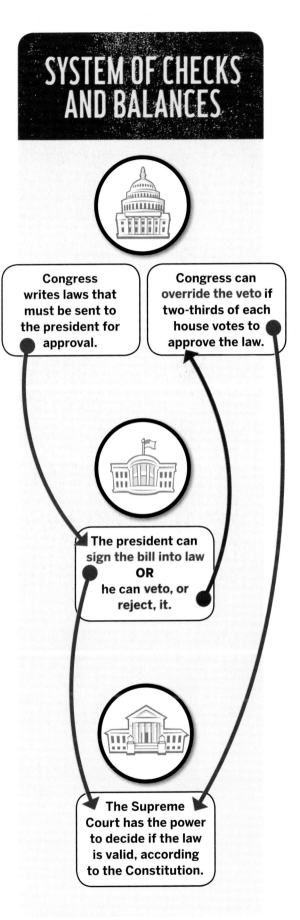

SYSTEM OF CHECKS AND BALANCES

Congress writes laws that must be sent to the president for approval.

Congress can override the veto if two-thirds of each house votes to approve the law.

The president can sign the bill into law **OR** he can veto, or reject, it.

The Supreme Court has the power to decide if the law is valid, according to the Constitution.

The Legislative Branch: Lawmakers

The Constitution established the country as a democracy. Every single person gets to have a say in how the country is run. But America would never get anything done if all 300 million Americans voiced their opinions on every decision. That's where the members of Congress come in.

Congress is made up of two parts that check and balance each other. One part is the House of Representatives. Representatives are charged with making decisions that are best for the people in their home states. California, the state with the biggest population, has 53 representatives. Wyoming, where the fewest people live, has just one. In total there are 435 representatives for all 50 states.

The other part of Congress is the Senate. There are two senators representing every state. The states have the same power in the Senate, so small states can't be bullied by big ones who have more representatives.

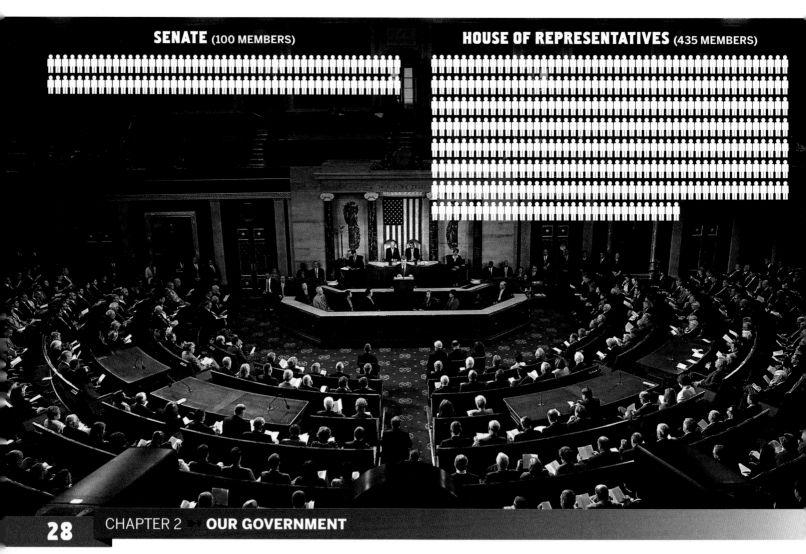

SENATE (100 MEMBERS)

HOUSE OF REPRESENTATIVES (435 MEMBERS)

HOW A BILL BECOMES A LAW

Every law in the United States starts as a bill. It often has to travel a winding road to become a law. This chart shows the straightest route a bill can take.

1
THE BILL IS INTRODUCED.
A member of Congress introduces the bill to the Senate or the House of Representatives. If there is enough support for the idea, then the bill goes to a committee for review.

2
THE COMMITTEE WEIGHS IN.
If the committee votes yes on the bill, the bill is sent back to the original house (House of Representatives or Senate) for debate.

3
THE ORIGINAL HOUSE CONSIDERS THE BILL.
The House of Representatives or Senate debates the bill. If members vote yes, the bill is sent to the other house.

4
THE OTHER HOUSE CONSIDERS THE BILL.
The other house debates and votes.

5a IF THERE ARE CHANGES...

THE BILL GOES BACK TO THE ORIGINAL HOUSE.
The original house votes whether to approve the changes.

5b IF THERE ARE NO CHANGES...

THE BILL GOES TO THE PRESIDENT.
If the president signs the bill, then it becomes a law. If the president vetoes the bill, it can still become a law, but only if two-thirds of the House and Senate vote to approve it.

The Executive Branch: Law Enforcers

Ronald Reagan was the 40th U.S. president.

The president of the United States has many responsibilities. He or she is the top officer in the military. He meets with leaders of other countries and makes important deals. He also decides which of Congress's bills to sign into law. The president chooses a team that helps him get these jobs done. His right-hand man (or woman) is the vice president. The vice president's biggest job is to be ready to serve as president if necessary. Fifteen other close advisors help the president make the hundreds of decisions he faces every day. These 15 people are the president's Cabinet.

Each Cabinet member is in charge of a department with its own mission and thousands of employees. The secretary of defense oversees the military, making sure Americans are safe at home and abroad. The secretary of education is like the school principal for the country, overseeing all of America's public schools. There are also departments for preventing disease, printing money, and making sure our food is safe to eat.

The most famous house in the United States is at 1600 Pennsylvania Avenue in Washington, D.C. This is where the president and his family live. George Washington picked the spot for this grand house, but it wasn't built in time for him to live there. So John Adams was the first president to make his bed in this mansion. In 1814, the White House was burned down in a war. It took three years to rebuild and, since then, the White House has been home to every president. Over the years, presidents added new rooms and wings. Today the White House is big enough to have 132 rooms, 35 bathrooms, 412 doors, 147 windows, and three elevators!

This seal is the official symbol of the president of the United States. The eagle holds in one talon an olive branch with 13 leaves, representing peace. The other talon holds 13 arrows representing war, because America will defend itself if necessary. The number 13 honors the original 13 colonies. And the Latin words above the eagle—"E Pluribus Unum"— mean "out of many, one." These words are a reminder that many people and states make up a single country, the United States of America.

The president works in the Oval Office, which is named for its shape.

The Judicial Branch: Law Referees

THE SUPREME COURT IN 2010

BACK ROW, FROM LEFT: Sonia Sotomayor, Stephen Breyer, Samuel Alito, Elena Kagan
FRONT ROW, FROM LEFT: Clarence Thomas, Antonin Scalia*, Chief Justice John Roberts, Anthony Kennedy, Ruth Bader Ginsburg

*died in 2016

C ourt cases that are hard to decide can make it all the way to the Supreme Court, the highest in the land. Supreme Court rulings must be followed by all the lower courts and its decisions affect the entire country.

The main job of the nine justices on the Supreme Court is to decide whether laws agree with the Constitution. Everyone agrees that the Constitution is important, but many argue over how the words in that document should be understood. Times have changed. New questions come up that the Founding Fathers didn't even think about in a time before cars or TVs or airplanes had been invented. Sometimes the judicial branch has to update old ideas for modern times.

Segregation, for example, was once legal. In the 1950s, school officials around the United States made black children and white children attend different schools. But in 1954, the Supreme Court ruled that this was wrong because the Constitution says all people have to be treated equally. Children of different races should be able to go to the same schools and get the same education.

It took years for schools to integrate after the Supreme Court's ruling. Here, picketers protest the segregation of public schools in St. Louis, Missouri, in 1962.

For hundreds of years, Lady Justice has been a symbol of our legal system. She is usually shown with a sword and scales. The scales represent the weighing of an argument. The sword stands for the power of justice. Some depictions include a blindfold, meaning that justice treats all people the same, no matter what they look like, whether they are rich or poor, strong or weak.

How Elections Work

First Lady Michelle Obama and President Barack Obama celebrate his re-election in Chicago, Illinois, in 2012.

Men and women running for an elected office are called candidates. They give speeches telling people why they're best for the job. They march in parades, shake people's hands, and take part in debates. This is called campaigning. At the end of the campaign, the American people vote, and the person with the most votes usually wins the office. (See "Who Picks the President?" for an exception to this rule.)

There are all kinds of elected offices. Mayors are elected officials in charge of cities. Governors are elected officials in charge of states. Even some judges are elected. But the biggest election is the one for the president. Every four years on the first Tuesday in November, Americans go to the polls to cast their votes.

All U.S. citizens get the right to vote on their 18th birthday. Some choose not to exercise this right. They're missing their chance to have a say in how our government works.

Going to the Polls (2012)

Could have voted: **235 million**

Chose to vote: **129 million**

Who Picks the President?

The U.S. Constitution established the Electoral College. Some of the Founding Fathers wanted Congress to pick the president, while others wanted citizens to decide. The Electoral College was a compromise. Each state is assigned a number of electoral votes, based on its population. A candidate needs 270 of 538 total electoral votes to become president. In 48 states, the winner of the popular vote gets all of that state's electoral votes. In Maine and Nebraska, the electoral votes can be split between the candidates. The map shows the Election 2012 results.

Key
- Barack Obama
- Mitt Romney

IT'S A PARTY!

In America, there are two main political parties: Democrats and Republicans. Members of a political party often share the same values and ideas. Politicians don't have to join a party, but they usually do. It's like joining a team. Democrats help one another get elected and help turn one another's bills into laws. Republicans do the same. Each party can only choose one candidate to run for president and an election usually comes down to a battle between one Democrat and one Republican. The symbol of the Republican party is the elephant and the symbol of the Democratic party is the donkey. A cartoonist created these symbols more than 100 years ago and they stuck!

Have A Say

Protesters call on the U.S. government to stop sending immigrants who don't have the right documents back to their home countries.

Americans hold differing opinions about how our government should run and what America's role in the world should be. No matter what the president or lawmakers do, there will always be some people who are happy and others who are unhappy.

When people aren't happy with the government, they have the right to petition. A petition is a written statement asking for change. Let's say some people want to protect trees that are going to be cut down. They can ask the government to step in. Anyone who supports the effort can sign the petition. The signatures are presented to the government as proof that people care. The government can either do what the people have requested or explain why it won't.

TELL IT TO THE PRESIDENT!

Barack Obama, who was first elected president in 2008, started a website where Americans can submit online petitions for the first time in history. So far, there have been thousands of submissions at petitions. whitehouse.gov. Most are serious, such as those asking the government to help cure diseases, or to allow more people to become citizens. A few requests are silly, such as one that asked the government to give everyone in America a lollipop on the day after Christmas. The White House promises to respond to any petition that gets 100,000 signatures in 30 days.

1.

Go to **petitions.whitehouse.gov.**

🔒 petitions.whitehouse.gov

2.

Create a petition for others to sign.

We petition the Administration to:

Make chocolate milk mandatory in all school cafeterias.

1,500 signatures   **FIND OUT MORE**

3.

If the petition gets 100,000 signatures in 30 days, the White House will respond.

"We the People" by the Numbers

 **19,507,060*** users

 **411,546*** petitions

 **27,771,912*** signatures

*Numbers as of March 2016

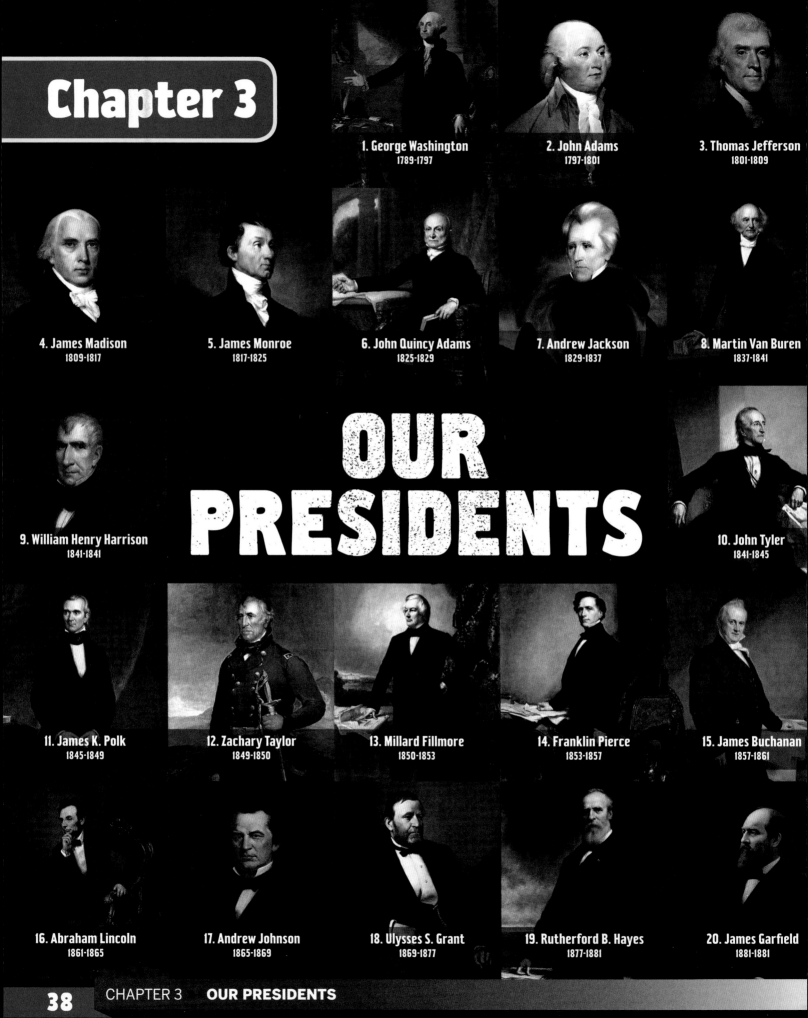

Chapter 3

OUR PRESIDENTS

1. George Washington
1789-1797

2. John Adams
1797-1801

3. Thomas Jefferson
1801-1809

4. James Madison
1809-1817

5. James Monroe
1817-1825

6. John Quincy Adams
1825-1829

7. Andrew Jackson
1829-1837

8. Martin Van Buren
1837-1841

9. William Henry Harrison
1841-1841

10. John Tyler
1841-1845

11. James K. Polk
1845-1849

12. Zachary Taylor
1849-1850

13. Millard Fillmore
1850-1853

14. Franklin Pierce
1853-1857

15. James Buchanan
1857-1861

16. Abraham Lincoln
1861-1865

17. Andrew Johnson
1865-1869

18. Ulysses S. Grant
1869-1877

19. Rutherford B. Hayes
1877-1881

20. James Garfield
1881-1881

21. Chester A. Arthur
1881-1885

22. Grover Cleveland
1885-1889

23. Benjamin Harrison
1889-1893

24. Grover Cleveland
1893-1897

25. William McKinley
1897-1901

26. Theodore Roosevelt
1901-1909

27. William Howard Taft
1909-1913

28. Woodrow Wilson
1913-1921

29. Warren G. Harding
1921-1923

30. Calvin Coolidge
1923-1929

31. Herbert Hoover
1929-1933

32. Franklin D. Roosevelt
1933-1945

33. Harry S. Truman
1945-1953

34. Dwight D. Eisenhower
1953-1961

35. John F. Kennedy
1961-1963

36. Lyndon B. Johnson
1963-1969

37. Richard M. Nixon
1969-1974

38. Gerald R. Ford
1974-1977

39. James Carter
1977-1981

40. Ronald Reagan
1981-1989

41. George H.W. Bush
1989-1993

42. William J. Clinton
1993-2001

43. George W. Bush
2001-2009

44. Barack Obama
2009-2017

Who Can Be President?

Kids are often told that they could grow up to be president. But there are a few rules about who is allowed to run for the most powerful elected office in the country.

In order to become president,

* You must be a natural-born citizen.
* You must have lived in the United States for at least 14 years.
* You must be at least 35 years old.

All presidents must have at least one other thing in common. They have to be able to persuade the American people to vote for them!

Whatever plane the president is on is called Air Force One. The plane he usually uses has three stories, including dining areas that can seat 100 people and an operating room. If there is an emergency, the plane has everything the president needs to run the government from the sky. It can even refuel in midair.

HELLO
my name is

POTUS — Leader of the Free World commander-in-chief

The president goes by more than one name. As the top leader in the military, the president is known as the commander-in-chief. He is also called the Leader of the Free World. Sometimes people use the acronym POTUS, for president of the United States.

THE WORLD'S TOUGHEST JOB

The president has one of the coolest jobs and also one of the hardest. Presidents travel around the world on their own airplanes. They know secrets that no one else does. They're famous and many people admire them.

Most important, they have the power to shape the history of the country and the world. Presidents make life-or-death decisions, like whether America should send soldiers into wars. They work long days and can't go anywhere without bodyguards.

President James Polk once said, "The presidency is no bed of roses." President Martin Van Buren said that two days were the happiest of his life: the day he became president and the day he finished.

WHERE U.S. PRESIDENTS WERE BORN

Some states have produced a lot more presidents than other states (partly because some of those states have been around longer):

Virginia: 8
Ohio: 7
Massachusetts: 4
New York: 4
North Carolina: 2
Texas: 2
Vermont: 2
Arkansas: 1
Connecticut: 1
California: 1
Georgia: 1

Hawaii: 1
Illinois: 1
Iowa: 1
Kentucky: 1
Missouri: 1
Nebraska: 1
New Hampshire: 1
New Jersey: 1
Pennsylvania: 1
South Carolina: 1

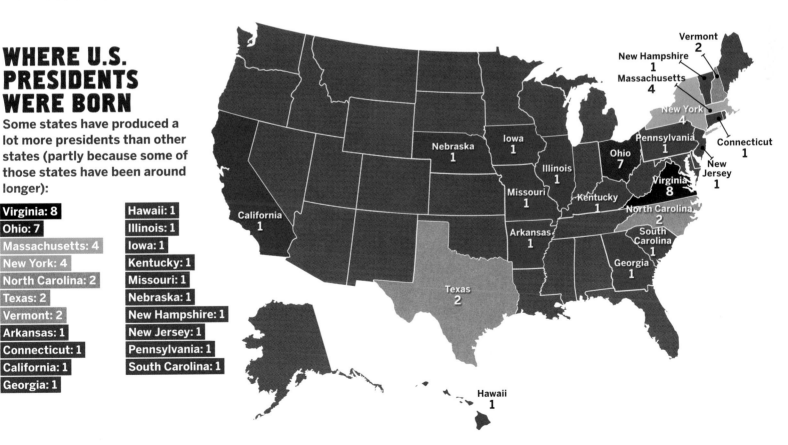

Vermont 2
New Hampshire 1
Massachusetts 4
New York 4
Connecticut 1
New Jersey 1
Pennsylvania 1
Ohio 7
Virginia 8
Nebraska 1
Iowa 1
Illinois 1
Missouri 1
Kentucky 1
North Carolina 2
South Carolina 1
Arkansas 1
Georgia 1
California 1
Texas 2
Hawaii 1

Leading Ladies

The wife of the president is known as the first lady. She plays an important role for the country.

In America's early days, the first lady was mostly in charge of running the White House. She would act as a hostess, decorator, and caretaker.

Over the years, first ladies have helped build good relations with leaders of other countries and acted as advisors to their husbands. They have been effective campaigners, too.

Many first ladies have championed causes, like teaching children to read and keeping them off drugs.

So far, there hasn't been a female president, so there's no rule about what her husband might be called. He could be a first man or a first gentleman. Maybe even a first dude!

FIGHTING FOR A CAUSE

LOUISA ADAMS, 1825-1829:
The wife of President John Quincy Adams was one of the first—but certainly not the last—to fight for women's rights. Women didn't win the right to vote for nearly 100 years after Louisa began serving as first lady.

ELLEN WILSON, 1913-1914:
When Ellen arrived in Washington, D.C., with her husband Woodrow Wilson, she found poor people living in terrible conditions. She inspired a bill to improve housing, known as "Ellen Wilson's bill." It became law in 1914.

ELEANOR ROOSEVELT, 1933-1945:
The wife of Franklin Roosevelt was a first lady longer than any other woman. She was a champion of women's rights her whole life. She also fought for human rights around the world.

JACKIE KENNEDY, 1961-1963:
Jackie Kennedy served as first lady for only two years. But in that short time, she inspired America with her love of the arts and history. She gave the White House a makeover, transforming it into a museum of American history.

LADY BIRD JOHNSON, 1963-1969:
The wife of Lyndon B. Johnson loved the outdoors. She fought to protect nature and make America more beautiful. Thanks to her efforts, important landmarks in America—like the Appalachian Trail— are protected by the federal government.

BETTY FORD, 1974-1977:
The wife of America's 38th president fought for women's rights. She also brought attention to the needs of the disabled and worked to help people recover from addiction.

NANCY REAGAN, 1981-1989:
"Just say no." That phrase became famous when Nancy Reagan was first lady. Her cause was keeping kids off drugs, and her slogan was used by thousands of groups working to keep kids healthy and safe.

HILLARY CLINTON, 1993-2001:
Before she was a presidential candidate, a New York senator, or secretary of state, Hillary Clinton was a first lady. In that role, she fought to help poor people get better medical care.

LAURA BUSH, 2001-2009:
The wife of President George W. Bush worked as a librarian and a school teacher. As first lady, she promoted literacy. She founded the National Book Festival which takes place each year in Washington, D.C.

MICHELLE OBAMA, 2009-2017:
Michelle Obama has worked to improve America's eating and exercise habits. Her slogan is "Let's Move." She once invited kids to the White House to break the world record for the most people doing jumping jacks in 24 hours.

Recent Presidents

O nly time will tell which presidents will be remembered as the greatest. Here is an introduction to the most recent presidents, whose place in history has yet to be decided.

From left to right: George H.W. Bush, Barack Obama, George W. Bush, and Bill Clinton.

BARACK OBAMA, 2009-2017
PRESIDENT #44

Age when he became president: 47
Hobbies: Playing basketball, cooking
His story: Barack Obama was born in Hawaii in 1961. His father was from Kenya, in Africa, and his mother was from Kansas. As president he fought to make health care affordable for all. He started his term when the economy was struggling and a lot of people were out of jobs. He worked to fix those problems.
Did You Know? He was the first president to sit for a 3-D portrait!

GEORGE W. BUSH, 2001-2009
PRESIDENT #43

Age when he became president: 54
Hobbies: Painting, fishing
His story: Soon after George W. Bush was elected president, there was a terrible tragedy. On September 11, 2001, terrorists crashed airplanes into the World Trade Center towers in New York City, killing thousands. Bush spent his time as president fighting terrorists and working to make the country safer.
Did You Know? He was the second president to have a father who had also been president. His father, George H.W. Bush, was the 41st president.

BILL CLINTON, 1993-2001
PRESIDENT #42

Age when he became president: 46
Hobbies: Playing the saxophone, jogging
His story: Bill Clinton helped improve the American economy (the country's measure of wealth and resources) when times were tough. By his last two years in office, the country enjoyed a budget surplus. People who had lost their jobs had gotten them back, and fewer people were severely poor. He left the presidency with high approval ratings.
Did You Know? After serving as first lady, his wife, Hillary Clinton, became a Senator of New York and ran for president in 2008. She didn't win, but President Obama appointed her secretary of state. She ran again for president in 2016.

GEORGE H.W. BUSH, 1989-1993
PRESIDENT #41

Age when he became president: 64
Hobbies: Playing horseshoes, skydiving
His story: Before he became president, George H.W. Bush fought in World War II and won an award for his bravery. He also served in Congress and as vice president. During his time as president, war broke out in the Middle East. Bush sent American soldiers to help defend Kuwait against its bigger neighbor, Iraq. The war ended in just a few weeks.
Did You Know? He went skydiving at the age of 90. His parachute was red, white, and blue.

History's Superstars

Historians have ranked past presidents from not-so-great to greatest. The next pages will take a closer look at the presidents who historians say have made the biggest imprints on American history. Meet the superstars!

GEORGE WASHINGTON, 1789-1797
PRESIDENT #1

Age when he became president: 57
Born in: Virginia
He was best known for: leading the colonists to victory in the Revolutionary War and serving as the first president of the United States.
Did You Know? He declined to serve a third term as president.

JAMES K. POLK, 1845-1849
PRESIDENT #11

Age when he became president: 49
Born in: North Carolina
Best known for: expanding the size of the United States. He gained land that today makes up states including Texas, New Mexico, Oregon, and California. For the first time, America stretched from the Atlantic to the Pacific Ocean.
Did You Know? He was the only president who was born in North Carolina.

THOMAS JEFFERSON, 1801-1809
PRESIDENT #3

Age when he became president: 57
Born in: Virginia
Best known for: writing the Declaration of Independence.
Did You Know? He bought land from France that doubled the size of the U.S. The deal was known as the Louisiana Purchase. He got a sweet deal, paying less than 3¢ per acre! (An acre is almost the size of a football field.)

ABRAHAM LINCOLN, 1861-1865
PRESIDENT #16

Age when he became president: 52
Born in: Kentucky
Best known for: keeping the United States in one piece! When the southern states tried to secede from the country (meaning they would split from America and form their own country) Lincoln rallied northern troops and fought to stop them. In 1865, his side won the war.
Did You Know? Lincoln was assassinated by John Wilkes Booth, one of many southerners who were angry with him.

1800

WOODROW WILSON, 1913-1921
PRESIDENT #28

Age when he became president: 56
Born in: Virginia
Best known for: leading America and its allies to victory in World War I.
Did You Know? He made Mother's Day a national holiday in 1914. Wilson said the second Sunday in May should be a day to express love and respect for mothers across the country.

HARRY S. TRUMAN, 1945-1953
PRESIDENT #33

Age when he became president: 60
Born in: Missouri
Best known for: leading America and its allies to victory in World War II. After the war, he helped to rebuild Europe.
Did You Know? His middle name is just one letter. Both of his grandfathers had names starting with "S." His parents couldn't agree which name to give their son. They compromised and used "S."

THEODORE ROOSEVELT, 1901-1909
PRESIDENT #26

Age when he became president: 42
Born in: New York
Best known for: being a tough guy who loved nature. As president, he conserved many beautiful American lands, and doubled the number of National Parks.
Did You Know? In 1906, he became the first American to win the Nobel Peace Prize, for helping to bring about peace in the Russo-Japanese War.

FRANKLIN D. ROOSEVELT, 1933-1945
PRESIDENT #32

Age when he became president: 51
Born in: New York
Best known for: rescuing the country from the Great Depression of the 1930s, when many people lost their jobs and their life savings. He was also president when America entered World War II in 1941.
Did You Know? He was the only president to be elected four times!

DWIGHT D. EISENHOWER, 1953-1961
PRESIDENT #34

Age when he became president: 62
Born in: Texas
Best known for: leading fighters to victory as a general in World War II. As president, Eisenhower worked hard to avoid other wars. He also built America's highways.
Did You Know? He was the only president who served in World War I and World War II.

1900

History's Stars

Here are presidents many historians think were great, even though they didn't shape history quite as much as the superstars. Some of them achieved their greatest feats before they got to the White House.

JOHN ADAMS, 1797-1801
PRESIDENT #2

Age when he became president: 61
Born in: Massachusetts
Best known for: leading the charge for independence! After the Revolutionary War, Adams helped negotiate a peace treaty with Britain. He became the first vice president and the second president.
Did You Know? He was the first president to live in the White House.

JAMES MONROE, 1817-1825
PRESIDENT #5

Age when he became president: 58
Born in: Virginia
Best known for: a U.S. foreign policy called the Monroe Doctrine. It was a warning to countries in Europe to keep their hands off land in America.
Did You Know? He was the third president to die on the Fourth of July. John Adams and Thomas Jefferson also died on Independence Day, five years before.

JAMES MADISON, 1809-1817
PRESIDENT #4

Age when he became president: 57
Born in: Virginia
Best known for: being the "Father of the Constitution." In 1787, Madison was a leader in writing the Constitution, which set up the U.S. government. He proposed many of the ideas in the Bill of Rights (see page 24).
Did You Know? He was the only president whose face has appeared on a $5,000 bill!

JOHN QUINCY ADAMS, 1825-1829
PRESIDENT #6

Age when he became president: 57
Born in: Massachusetts
Best known for: being a diplomat. He was great at taking care of America's relationships with other countries.
Did You Know? He was the first president who was also the son of a president. His dad, John Adams, was the second president.

1800

GROVER CLEVELAND, 1885-1889 AND 1893-1897
PRESIDENT #22 AND #24

Age when he became president: 55
Born in: New Jersey
Best known for: being fair and saving money. He gave people jobs only if they earned them and refused to do favors that would cost the country big bucks.
Did You Know? He was the only president to have won, lost, and then won a presidential election again.

WILLIAM HOWARD TAFT, 1909-1913
PRESIDENT #27

Age when he became president: 51
Born in: Ohio
Best known for: his great understanding of the law. After he left office, he became a justice on the Supreme Court.
Did You Know? He was a big guy. He weighed as much as 300 pounds when he was president. By comparison, the Founding Father James Madison weighed only 100 pounds!

LYNDON B. JOHNSON, 1963-1969
PRESIDENT #36

Age when he became president: 55
Born in: Texas
He was best known for: signing into law the Civil Rights Act of 1964, which outlaws discrimination based on gender, race, or religion.
Did You Know? He was the only president who didn't take the oath of office in Washington, D.C. After President Kennedy was assassinated in Texas, Johnson had to quickly take his place.

WILLIAM MCKINLEY, 1897-1901
PRESIDENT #25

Age when he became president: 54
Born in: Ohio
Best known for: leading the country to victory in the Spanish-American war and winning the territories of Guam, Puerto Rico, and the Philippines. Today, Guam and Puerto Rico are still U.S. territories.
Did You Know? He had a pet parrot.

JOHN F. KENNEDY, 1961-1963
PRESIDENT #35

Age when he became president: 43
Born in: Massachusetts
Best known for: being the youngest candidate to be elected president. He was also the youngest to die. Kennedy was shot and killed in Dallas, Texas, before he had served three years as president.
Did You Know? He was the first Catholic president.

RONALD REAGAN, 1981-1989
PRESIDENT #40

Age when he became president: 69
Born in: Illinois
Best known for: his speeches. People called him "the great communicator." Reagan struck a deal with the Soviet Union (today called Russia) to reduce each country's supply of nuclear weapons.
Did You Know? He loved jelly beans.

1900

Chapter 4

Visitors to the U.S.A. are treated to miles of natural and historic landmarks. Catch the view from the Statue of Liberty's crown in New York. Hike the Grand Canyon in Arizona. Meet four presidents at Mount Rushmore in South Dakota. Zip across the Golden Gate Bridge in California. Take a trip from coast to coast!

TOUR THE 50 STATES

Fall into New England

The states in the Northeast are called New England because many of the early settlers came from England. These are some of the oldest states in the U.S., known for cold weather, brightly colored foliage, and the shellfish that fishermen catch off their coastlines.

Maine
Nickname: The Pine Tree State
State mammal: moose
Claims to fame: Maine has a rocky coastline dotted with lighthouses. Fishing is a big industry, and the state is especially famous for its lobster. Maine also leads the country in growing blueberries.

New Hampshire
Nickname: The Granite State. Granite is a type of rock common in the state.
State insect: ladybug
Claims to fame: New Hampshire is covered in trees, lakes, and ponds. Winters are long and cold. Visitors travel to the state to explore the White Mountains, and to see its old-fashioned covered bridges.

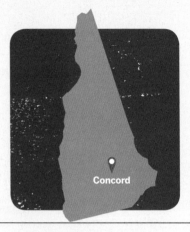

Vermont
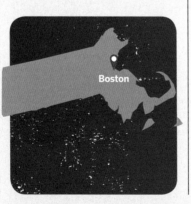

Nickname: The Green Mountain State
State tree: sugar maple. Maple syrup is made from the tree's sap.
Claims to fame: Vermont produces more maple syrup than any other state. The state is also known for its ski resorts and snowboarding. Lake Champlain is rumored to have a monster living in it named Champ. Don't worry, it's just a legend.

Massachusetts
Nickname: The Bay State
State folk hero: Johnny Appleseed, who was born in Massachusetts, became famous for planting apple trees around the country.
Claims to fame: The pilgrims landed here. Its capital, Boston, is the largest city in New England. The state is also known for its seafood and sandy coastline. The Bay State's most popular sports team is the Boston Red Sox.

Rhode Island

Nickname: The Ocean State
State shell: quahog (KOH-hawg). A quahog is a thick-shelled clam that fisherman gather off the state's coast.
Claims to fame: Rhode Island is the smallest state, about 1,000 square miles. It could fit into Texas about 200 times! Tourists travel to the tiny state for its quaint seaside towns and the giant mansions of Newport.

Connecticut
Nickname: The Constitution State. Some historians claim the state's founders wrote the first constitution in North America.
State animal: sperm whale. Whaling was once a big industry in the state. People used whale oil for lighting lamps.
Claims to fame: Connecticut is known for its colonial villages. It's also home to one of the largest collections of dinosaur tracks in the country.

Mosey Around the Mid-Atlantic

T he Mid-Atlantic states make up the middle part of the U.S. that borders the Atlantic Ocean. It's a diverse region, full of big cities, little farms and important businesses.

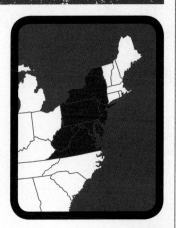

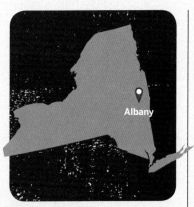

New Jersey
Nickname: The Garden State
State animal: horse
Claims to fame: Tourists visit the state's seaside boardwalks lined with carnival rides and arcades. New Jersey has lots of forests and farms, too. The state is the birthplace of many inventions, like a lightbulb for the masses and the TV dinner. No wonder New Jersey has its own inventors hall of fame!

New York
Nickname: The Empire State
State fruit: apple
Claims to fame: With 8.4 million residents, New York City has the biggest population of any U.S. city. The "Big Apple" is a center for art, culture, and business. People call it "the city that never sleeps." New York state is also home to dairy farms, apple orchards, and Niagara Falls.

Pennsylvania
Nickname: The Keystone State. A keystone is the one stone at the top of an arch that keeps all the other stones from falling.
State dog: Great Dane
Claims to fame: The Declaration of Independence and the U.S. Constitution were ratified in the state's largest city, Philadelphia.

Delaware
Nickname: The First State. Delaware was the first state to adopt the U.S. Constitution.
State dessert: peach pie
Claims to fame: Because of business-friendly laws, thousands of companies are based in Delaware. The state is also home to the oldest log cabins built in the United States. And it has only three counties—the fewest of any state.

Maryland
Nickname: The Free State, the Old Line State
State sport: jousting
Claims to fame: Maryland is known for its waterfronts, blue crabs, and sailing. Many people who work for the U.S. government live in Maryland, because it's close to Washington, D.C. The president even has a country house there, Camp David.

Virginia
Nickname: Mother of Presidents. Virginia is the birthplace of more presidents (eight) than any other state.
State dog: foxhound
Claims to fame: The Pentagon, headquarters to the Army, Navy, Air Force, and Marines, is located here. The headquarters of the Central Intelligence Agency (CIA) are also located in Virginia.

West Virginia
Nickname: Mountain State
State animal: black bear
Claims to fame: West Virginia got its nickname from the Appalachian Mountains extending along the state's eastern border. Appalachian music uses fiddles and twanging banjos. The land is full of coal, which miners have been digging for decades.

Take a Rest in the Midwest

T he Midwest's fertile soil produces abundant crops of wheat, oats, and corn. That's why the region is known as the country's "breadbasket." Stomachs around the U.S. owe the Midwest a debt of gratitude!

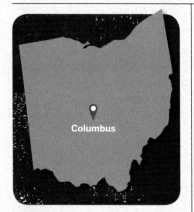

Columbus

Ohio

Nickname: The Buckeye State. The name comes from a tree that grows in Ohio.
State fruit: pawpaw
Claims to fame: Ohio is an important place for presidential candidates. It's known as a bellwether state, meaning that the candidate Ohioans vote for often wins the election. Visitors can rock out at the Rock and Roll Hall of Fame in Cleveland. The first professional baseball game was played here, too!

Indiana

Nickname: The Hoosier State. A Hoosier is someone from Indiana. The nickname has been used since the 1800s, but no one is sure what it means.
State motto: "The Crossroads of America"
Claims to fame: Farmers across Indiana grow popcorn, tomatoes, and peppermint. The capital city is famous for the Indianapolis 500 car race. Professional drivers race 500 miles around a track. The fastest time ever was 2 hours and 40 minutes.

Indianapolis

Springfield

Illinois

Nickname: Prairie State
State grass: big bluestem
Claims to fame: The biggest city in the Midwest is Chicago, Illinois. It's known for comedy, blues music, impressive skyscrapers, and pizza that's three inches thick. Before he was president, Abraham Lincoln served as a lawmaker in Illinois. That's why the state has a second nickname: The Land of Lincoln. Outside Chicago, the land is covered by big grasslands called prairies.

Michigan

Nickname: The Wolverine State. A wolverine is a small furry mammal in the weasel family. Also Great Lakes State.
State bird: American robin
Claims to fame: Michigan is the only state made up of two peninsulas, which are strips of land surrounded by water on three sides. In fact, no one in the state lives more than 100 miles from the water! Michigan is well known for making cars. Its biggest city, Detroit, is sometimes called the Automotive Capital of the World.

Lansing

Wisconsin

Nickname: The Badger State. A badger is a mammal in the weasel family.
State symbol of peace: dove
Claims to fame: Cheese! Wisconsin produces so many dairy products that its residents are sometimes called "Cheeseheads." In the winter, it gets so cold that people race cars and motorcycles on frozen lakes.

Minnesota

Nickname: The North Star State
State sport: ice hockey
Claims to fame: Minnesota is one of the coldest states. That may be why Minnesotans can't get enough ice hockey. When it's warm enough, visitors and locals love to canoe and boat on the state's many lakes. Despite the state's nickname, Land of 10,000 Lakes, there are actually more than 15,000 lakes in Minnesota!

North Dakota

Nickname: Peace Garden State. The Peace Garden sits across the U.S.-Canada border. The countries share it, showing their friendship.
State fruit: chokecherry
Claims to fame: North Dakota is a cold place with lots of open land and few people. Locals live in rural towns and on farms, where they drill for oil, raise turkeys, and grow sunflower seeds.

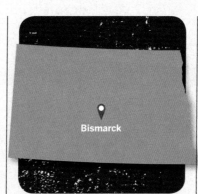

South Dakota

Nickname: The Mount Rushmore State
State fossil: Triceratops
Claims to fame: South Dakota is home to Mount Rushmore. It's also the site of the Badlands, rocky landscapes that look like they're from another planet. About 10% of the state's population is Native American, many from the Sioux Tribe.

Iowa

Nickname: The Hawkeye State. That name was chosen in honor of Native Americans, some of whom had names like "Black Hawk."
State flower: wild rose
Claims to fame: Iowa produces more corn, eggs, and pork than any other state in the nation. It is part of America's "breadbasket," the states that grow much of our country's food. It's also the birthplace of Otto Rohwedder, the inventor of the first bread-slicing machine in 1928.

Nebraska

Nickname: The Cornhusker State
State bird: meadowlark
Claims to fame: Like Iowa, Nebraska is part of the breadbasket. Almost the whole state is covered in farmland and plains. And it's some of the best farmland in the entire country. Many farmers raise cattle and the capital city, Omaha, is famous for its steaks. Nebraska was even called the "Beef State" for a while!

Kansas

Nickname: The Sunflower State
State animal: American buffalo
Claims to fame: The exact center of the United States (not counting Alaska and Hawaii) is in Kansas. This area is called the Heartland, because it's like the nation's heart in the middle of its body. Kansas grows more wheat than any other state. In its Wild West days, cowboys would have showdowns and shootouts in the streets.

Missouri

Nickname: The Show-Me State. The name came from a Missouri lawmaker who said he didn't believe fancy talk—to make him believe something, people had to show him.
State musical instrument: fiddle
Claims to fame: Missouri is home to the Gateway Arch, a 600-foot "doorway" that was built to honor pioneers who explored unknown lands in the West. Missouri was also the birthplace of humorist Mark Twain.

March Through the Mountains

S tates in the west are known for their high peaks. Early settlers there were tough people who were ready for adventure! Today people still travel to the West to explore the wilderness.

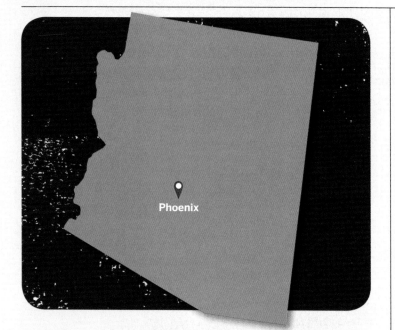

Phoenix

Arizona
Nickname: The Grand Canyon State
State gem: turquoise
Claims to fame: Arizona is home to the Grand Canyon. Over millions of years, the Colorado River carved out this vast, colorful canyon in the rocks. The country's largest cactus plants, called saguaro (sah-wah-ruh), grow in Arizona's Sonoran Desert. The tallest saguaro ever towered 78 feet.

New Mexico
Nickname: The Land of Enchantment
State aircraft: hot air balloon
Claims to fame: The state is home to mountains of white sands, pink rocks, and deep caverns. Every year people from all over the world fly their colorful hot air balloons in Albuquerque, a New Mexico city known as the "Balloon capital of the world."

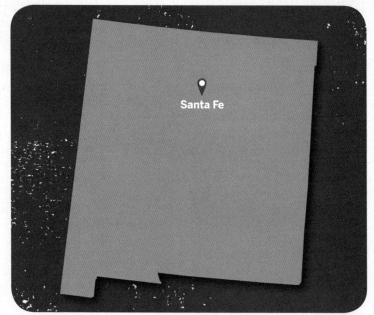

Santa Fe

Nevada

Nickname: The Silver State
State animal: desert bighorn sheep
Claims to fame: Nevada is home to impressive mountains and barren deserts. On the border the state shares with Arizona is the Hoover Dam. It uses water to make electricity and was one of the biggest things man had ever made when it was built in 1935.

Colorado

Nickname: The Centennial State
State sports: snowboarding and skiing
Claims to fame: Colorado is home to world-class ski resorts in the Rocky Mountains. The land is dotted with canyons, sand dunes, and bright blue lakes. This rocky state is also home to America's highest town. Leadville, a small town of 2,000 people, is 10,000 feet above sea level.

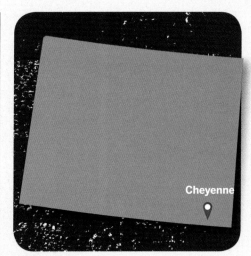

Wyoming

Nickname: The Cowboy State
State sport: rodeo
Claims to fame: Wyoming is huge, but it has the smallest population of any state. The land has long been home to ranchers and cowboys. In fact, there are more cattle than people in the state! Wyoming is also home to Yellowstone National Park—America's first national park.

Idaho

Nickname: The Gem State
State vegetable: potato
Claims to fame: The last time you had French fries, you were probably eating potatoes grown in Idaho. Farmers grow 25 different types of potatoes and champion them as the finest spuds in the world. Visitors travel to the state to ski, hike, and see the "craters of the moon," black fields of lava that came out of volcanoes thousands of years ago.

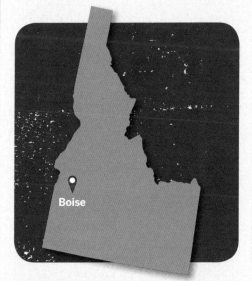

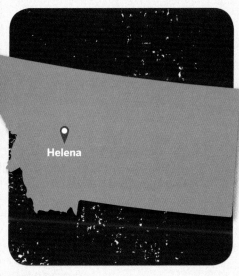

Montana

Nickname: The Treasure State
State animal: grizzly bear
Claims to fame: Like Wyoming, Montana is a huge state with a small population. It's famous for its views that seem to go on forever. The land is wild and green, home to animals like grizzly bears. In the north, Montana is home to Glacier National Park, land cold enough for mountains of ice to stay frozen!

Utah

Nickname: The Beehive State. The people in the state chose this nickname because they believe the bee is a hard worker, just like them.
State insect: European honeybee
Claims to fame: Utah is home to the country's biggest population of Mormons. They practice a religion that was founded in America in 1830. Mysterious landscapes of tall thin rocks called "hoodoos" can be found here.

Pass Time in the Pacific

The Pacific States border the Pacific Ocean in the west. These states are home to some of America's tallest mountains and trees. Technology companies like Apple, Google, and Facebook also make their homes here in one of the wealthiest areas of our country, Silicon Valley, in northern California.

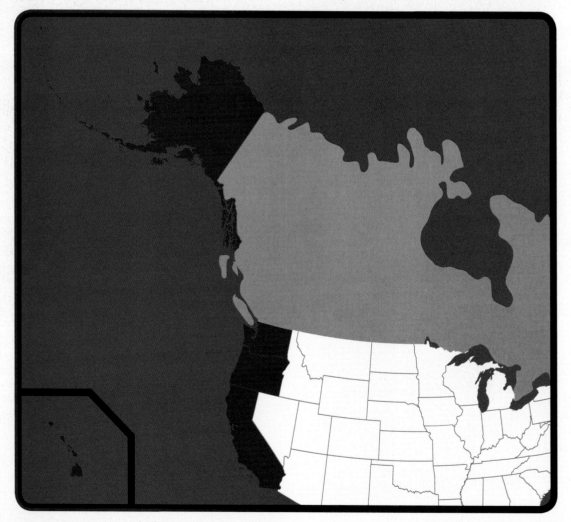

Olympia

Oregon

Nickname: The Beaver State
State fruit: pear
Claims to fame: If your family puts up a Christmas tree, it might have been chopped down in Oregon. This state grows more Christmas trees than any other. Oregon is also home to Crater Lake. It was formed when a volcano collapsed and is famous for its deep blue color. Also famous is the 2,000-mile Oregon Trail. In the 1800s, pioneers risked their lives traveling west to Oregon from Missouri.

Salem

Sacramento

Washington

Nickname: The Evergreen State
State fruit: apple. Washington grows more apples than any other state.
Claims to fame: Washington is home to some of the country's biggest, baddest mountains. Mount St. Helens is still an active volcano. It spewed the deadliest eruption in American history, in 1980. Visitors can check out the state's biggest city, Seattle, from a 600-foot tower called the Space Needle.

California

Nickname: The Golden State
State motto: "Eureka!"
Claims to fame: People rushed to California in 1849 in search of gold, and when they found it, they'd yell "Eureka!" Today, farmers grow so many fruits and vegetables that one valley is called "the salad bowl of the world." Actors seeking fame go to Hollywood. And nature-loving visitors go to California to see the famous redwood trees, the tallest in the world. One is 379 feet tall!

Juneau

Alaska

Nickname: The Last Frontier
State sport: dog mushing
Claims to fame: Alaska is the biggest state, twice the size of Texas. It's home to America's tallest mountains and biggest oil wells. Some Alaskan towns are so far north that they don't get any sunlight in the wintertime. One town stays dark for 65 days straight! Alaska is also home to Native Americans known as Inuits. It's so cold there, Inuits have come up with 100 words for different types of snow.

Honolulu

Hawaii

Nickname: The Aloha State
State mammal: monk seal
Claims to fame: Hawaii is the only U.S. state made up of islands. Surfing is a popular pastime. The state is still home to native Hawaiian people who lived here long before the state became part of America. Some of them still perform traditional dances like the hula. The state has two official languages: English and Hawaiian. "Aloha" is Hawaiian for "Hello!" and "Goodbye!"

Come to the Capital!

The capital of the United States isn't a state at all. It's an independent district called Washington, D.C. *D.C.* stands for District of Columbia. In the country's early days, other cities served as the capital. New York City was first, and then Philadelphia. Washington, D.C., became the capital in 1790. Check out some of the sites that make D.C. famous.

THE LINCOLN MEMORIAL

This giant monument honors the 16th president, Abraham Lincoln. The sculpture of him is 19 feet tall.

THE WASHINGTON MONUMENT

This memorial was built to honor the first president, George Washington. The 555-foot-tall structure is the tallest in Washington, D.C. By law, no building in the capital can be taller.

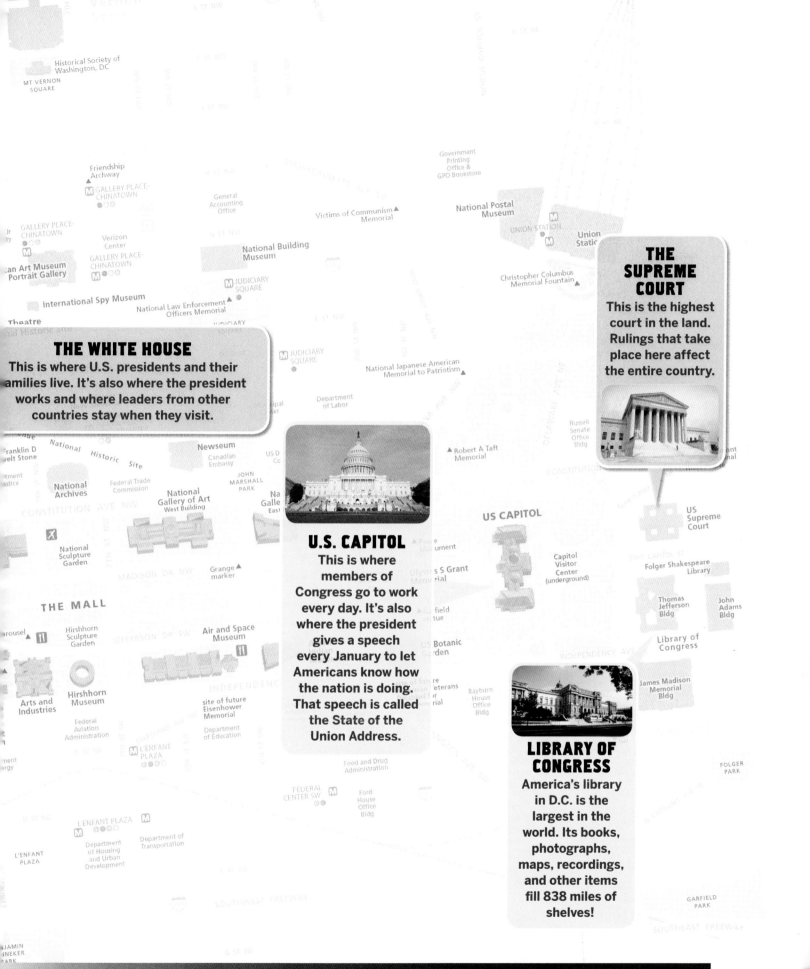

THE WHITE HOUSE
This is where U.S. presidents and their amilies live. It's also where the president works and where leaders from other countries stay when they visit.

THE SUPREME COURT
This is the highest court in the land. Rulings that take place here affect the entire country.

U.S. CAPITOL
This is where members of Congress go to work every day. It's also where the president gives a speech every January to let Americans know how the nation is doing. That speech is called the State of the Union Address.

LIBRARY OF CONGRESS
America's library in D.C. is the largest in the world. Its books, photographs, maps, recordings, and other items fill 838 miles of shelves!

Historical Society of Washington, DC
MT VERNON SQUARE
Friendship Archway
GALLERY PLACE-CHINATOWN
GALLERY PLACE-CHINATOWN
Verizon Center
GALLERY PLACE-CHINATOWN
an Art Museum Portrait Gallery
International Spy Museum
Theatre
al Historic Site
General Accounting Office
National Building Museum
JUDICIARY SQUARE
National Law Enforcement Officers Memorial
JUDICIARY
JUDICIARY SQUARE
Victims of Communism Memorial
National Japanese American Memorial to Patriotism
Department of Labor
Government Printing Office & GPO Bookstore
National Postal Museum
UNION STATION
Union Static
Christopher Columbus Memorial Fountain
Russell Senate Office Bldg
National Historic Site
Franklin D velt Stone
stice
National Archives
Federal Trade Commission
Newseum
Canadian Embassy
US D Co
JOHN MARSHALL PARK
Na Galle East
Robert A Taft Memorial
nt al
National Gallery of Art West Building
CONSTITUTION AVE NW
CONSTITUTION
National Sculpture Garden
MADISON DR NW
Grange marker
US CAPITOL
Capitol Visitor Center (underground)
US Supreme Court
Folger Shakespeare Library
Thomas Jefferson Bldg
John Adams Bldg
Library of Congress
THE MALL
arousel
Hirshhorn Sculpture Garden
JEFFERSON DR SW
Air and Space Museum
 field
Ulysses S Grant Memorial
INDEPENDENCE AVE
Arts and Industries
Hirshhorn Museum
Federal Aviation Administration
L'ENFANT PLAZA
site of future Eisenhower Memorial
Department of Education
INDEPENDENCE
US Botanic Garden
re e eterans r erial
Rayburn House Office Bldg
James Madison Memorial Bldg
ergy
nt
L'ENFANT PLAZA
L'ENFANT PLAZA
Department of Housing and Urban Development
Department of Transportation
Food and Drug Administration
FEDERAL CENTER SW
Ford House Office Bldg
FOLGER PARK
GARFIELD PARK
SOUTHWEST FREEWAY
SOUTHEAST FREEWAY
JAMIN NEKER PARK

Chapter 5

THE LAND

From sea to shining sea, our country is filled with wild beauty. You can visit snowcapped mountains in Alaska, tropical forests in Florida, arid deserts in the Southwest, and windswept plains west of the Mississippi River. Turn the page to discover the United States and all its varied landscapes.

Purple Mountain Majesties

> Denali is taller than 1,000 giraffes stacked head to hoof!

America's tallest mountains are in Alaska. The tallest, Denali, reaches 20,310 feet. It was formed by earthquakes 60 million years ago. The mountain is still growing, by about half a millimeter each year. The mountain was officially called "Mount McKinley" until 2015, when the U.S. Department of the Interior renamed it.

BEYOND ALASKA

America's ten tallest mountains are all in Alaska.
Here are the highest peaks that other states have to offer.

**California:
Mount Whitney
14,505 feet tall**

**Colorado:
Mount Elbert
14,440 feet tall**

**Washington:
Mount Rainier
14,411 feet tall**

**Florida:
Britton Hill
345 feet tall**

Scorching Hot Deserts

When we say Denali is 20,310 feet tall, we are saying the peak is 20,310 feet above sea level. Many places in the United States are lower than sea level. How low does the land go? About 282 feet below sea level, in a place known as Death Valley.

Death Valley, low land surrounded by mountains in the California desert, is one of the hottest places on earth. The highest temperature ever recorded on earth was in Death Valley in 1913, when the air heated up to 134 degrees!

In 1848, pioneers from all over the United States packed their belongings and headed west in wagons. They set out in search of gold and a better life. Along the way, some of these pioneers were trapped in the valley. They thought they were as good as dead. They survived, but the name they gave the dry, dusty place—Death Valley—lasted, too.

HIGHEST TEMPERATURE EVER RECORDED!

134°F

The Great Lakes

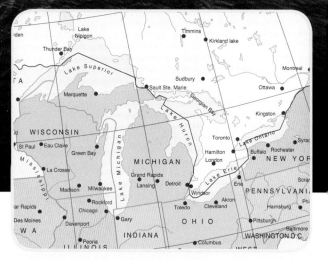

The Great Lakes are five giant lakes situated along the border of the United States and Canada. They're all connected by rivers and dams. A determined boater could paddle from Minnesota all the way to the Atlantic Ocean. Taken together, the Great Lakes are the biggest body of freshwater on the planet.

The Great Lakes are an important resource. More than 33 million people rely on them for drinking water. They are a big source of food with a yearly fishing catch of 110 million pounds. In the surrounding Great Lakes Basin, crops such as wheat, corn, barley, and oats grow. Plus, this huge water source provides cheap electricity and convenient shipping routes.

The lakes also provide a boost to tourism. More than 60 million people visit the Great Lakes each year to swim, fish, water ski, and kayak.

Here's a good way to remember the lakes' names: The first letter of each spells the word HOMES: Huron, Ontario, Michigan, Erie, Superior.

LAKE HURON is home to 30,000 little islands!

LAKE ONTARIO is the smallest Great Lake. It's named after a province in Canada.

LAKE MICHIGAN is the only Great Lake that isn't bordered by Canada.

LAKE ERIE is the shallowest of the lakes, usually the first to freeze over in winter.

LAKE SUPERIOR is the largest of the Great Lakes. It contains 3 quadrillion gallons of water, which could cover North and South America a foot deep.

The Mississippi River

The second longest river in the United States is the Mississippi. It's better known than the longest river—the Missouri—because it runs through the heart of the U.S., almost the entire way from Canada to the Gulf of Mexico.

The Mississippi River is an unofficial line that breaks up America into two parts. People will say, "That's the best BBQ this side of the Mississippi!" Or "You are the silliest nutcake west of the Mississippi."

The name *Mississippi* comes from an American Indian word meaning "big river" or "father of waters." The waterway starts in Minnesota and runs more than 2,300 miles through nine other states before emptying into the Gulf of Mexico. At its widest, the river is 11 miles across.

American Indians have lived along the Mississippi River for thousands of years. It provided them with a means of transportation, drinking water, and an abundance of freshwater fish. Later, the "Mighty Mississippi" became essential to the growth of our country. Traffic on the river includes barges and boats carrying everything from corn and grain to oil and coal. What's more, it is the main source of drinking water for millions.

Finding Forests

HOW TALL IS 400 FEET ANYWAY?

The tallest redwood is 379 feet tall. That's taller than the Statue of Liberty!

Conservationist John Muir once said that America is like a garden. From sea to sea, there are forests of trees. Some grow fruit. Some drop pinecones the size of small dogs. Some have droopy leaves. Some are homes for animals. Some get cut down and made into homes for people.

There are hundreds of different species of trees that make up America's forests. About one-third of the United States is considered forest land by the U.S. government! Muir Woods, in California, is one of those forests. It is home to some of the biggest trees in the world, known as redwoods. They are the tallest of all living things, with some reaching almost 400 feet into the air.

Americans can enjoy the towering trees in forests like Muir Woods thanks to environmentalists like Muir who fought to preserve our country's wild places.

Amber Waves of Grain

The middle of America is covered by the Great Plains. This enormous grassy patch stretches from Montana to the southern border of Texas, covering parts of 10 states.

In the 1930s, some parts of the Great Plains got so dry and windy that people called it the Dust Bowl. Terrible droughts and other problems caused millions of acres of farmland to dry up, turn to dust, and blow away. Huge dust storms, called black blizzards, came on suddenly and blanketed the land.

Today, the Great Plains are home to golden fields of wheat and corn. These grains feed the animals and farmers who keep our grocery shelves stocked and our kitchen cabinets full of food. Americans now call the Great Plains America's breadbasket for good reason.

The Grandest Canyon of Them All

Every year, five million people travel to Arizona to see the deep, rocky valley known as the Grand Canyon. They take in its otherworldly views, hike or ride mules on its trails, and raft in its river.

The Grand Canyon is 277 miles long, up to 18 miles across, and more than a mile deep. It took millions of years for a river, known today as the Colorado, to carve out the 6,000-foot deep canyon. Rock dating back nearly 2 billion years, the oldest exposed rock on earth, lies at the bottom.

Mind-Blowing Volcanoes

Kilauea (pronounced kill-uh-WAY-ah) is a 4,091-foot volcano in Hawaii that has been erupting continuously since 1983. Some say it's the most active volcano in the world. Its lava flows have added about 500 acres of new land to the island of Hawaii. In fact, millions of years ago the islands of Hawaii were formed by volcanoes.

Hawaii is not the only state in America that is home to volcanoes. Alaska has more than 130 of them. California, Oregon, and Washington are home to volcanoes, too.

WASHINGTON
RIVER OTTER

MONTANA
GRAY WOLF

NORTH DAKOTA
PRAIRIE RATTLESNAKE

OREGON
HUMPBACK WHALE

IDAHO
COUGAR

SOUTH DAKOTA
BLACK-FOOTED FERRET

MI...
PO...

WYOMING
BISON

NEBRASKA
JACKRABBIT

NEVADA
WILD HORSE

UTAH
PYGMY RABBIT

COLORADO
ELK

KANSAS
PRAIRIE DOG

CALIFORNIA
CALIFORNIA CONDOR

ARIZONA
DESERT TORTOISE

NEW MEXICO
JAGUAR

OKLAHOMA
WILD TURKE...

TEXAS
ANTELOPE

ALASKA
GRIZZLY BEAR

HAWAII
MONK SEAL

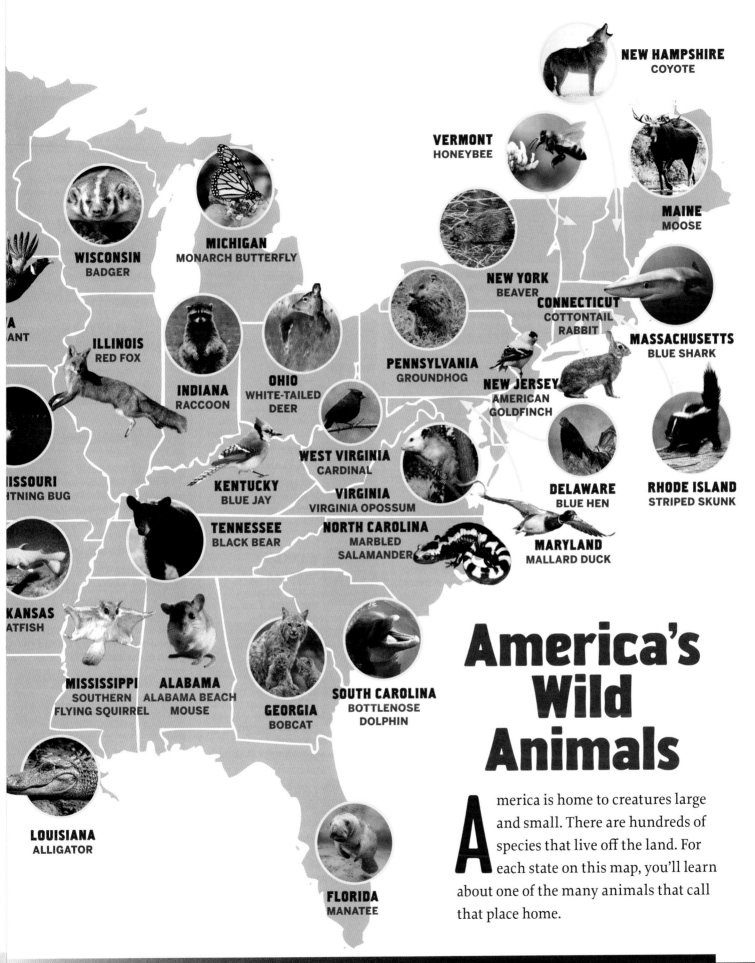

NEW HAMPSHIRE
COYOTE

VERMONT
HONEYBEE

MAINE
MOOSE

WISCONSIN
BADGER

MICHIGAN
MONARCH BUTTERFLY

NEW YORK
BEAVER

CONNECTICUT
COTTONTAIL
RABBIT

ILLINOIS
RED FOX

INDIANA
RACCOON

OHIO
WHITE-TAILED
DEER

PENNSYLVANIA
GROUNDHOG

NEW JERSEY
AMERICAN
GOLDFINCH

MASSACHUSETTS
BLUE SHARK

MISSOURI
...TNING BUG

WEST VIRGINIA
CARDINAL

KENTUCKY
BLUE JAY

VIRGINIA
VIRGINIA OPOSSUM

DELAWARE
BLUE HEN

RHODE ISLAND
STRIPED SKUNK

TENNESSEE
BLACK BEAR

NORTH CAROLINA
MARBLED
SALAMANDER

MARYLAND
MALLARD DUCK

...KANSAS
...TFISH

MISSISSIPPI
SOUTHERN
FLYING SQUIRREL

ALABAMA
ALABAMA BEACH
MOUSE

GEORGIA
BOBCAT

SOUTH CAROLINA
BOTTLENOSE
DOLPHIN

LOUISIANA
ALLIGATOR

FLORIDA
MANATEE

America's Wild Animals

A merica is home to creatures large and small. There are hundreds of species that live off the land. For each state on this map, you'll learn about one of the many animals that call that place home.

Chapter 6

COMING TO AMERICA

From 1892 to 1954, more than 12 million immigrants entered the United States through Ellis Island in New York Harbor. The Statue of Liberty stood ready to greet them as a symbol of freedom and democracy. Read on to learn about the people from all over the globe who make up this great country of ours.

Welcome to Ellis Island

This 1902 photo shows immigrants after their arrival by ship to Ellis Island in New York.

Beginning in 1892, the doorway to America was a place known as Ellis Island. This little island off the coast of New York was the place where ships full of people from other countries arrived after long, hard journeys across the sea. Many of these people left their old countries to escape war or starvation. Some had been treated badly because of their religion. They all hoped to discover better lives in the United States, a place known as the land of opportunity!

When these travelers arrived at Ellis Island, American officials would inspect their health to decide whether they could enter the United States. "Are you healthy?" the doctor might ask. "Do you have any rashes?" More than 12 million people, mostly from Europe, passed these tests and were sent on the final leg of their journey to the mainland. Others were turned away and put on ships to carry them back home. Ellis Island closed in the 1950s.

Today, about 40% of Americans can trace their family tree back to a relative who came through those halls many, many years ago to start a new life in the United States.

In 1892, a 15-year-old Irish girl named Annie Moore became the first person to enter the U.S. through Ellis Island. This statue of Annie and her two brothers is at her point of departure in Ireland. Another statue of the teen stands at Ellis Island, her port of arrival.

Meet Lady Liberty

TURN BOOK

The torch stands for liberty, or freedom. The flame is covered in thin sheets of 24-karat gold.

The seven points on Lady Liberty's crown represent the seven continents and the seven seas. Each point measures about 9 feet long and weighs as much as 150 pounds.

When the immigrants' ships arrived in New York Harbor, the Statute of Liberty greeted them. The statue was a gift from France in 1886 to celebrate the two countries' friendship. Inside, there are words from a poem called "The New Colossus" by Emma Lazarus that explain America's attitude about welcoming people from other lands. The last lines read,

"Give me your tired, your poor,
Your huddled masses yearning
*   to breathe free,*
The wretched refuse of your
*   teeming shore.*
Send these, the homeless,
*   tempest-tost to me*
I lift my lamp beside the golden
*   door!"*

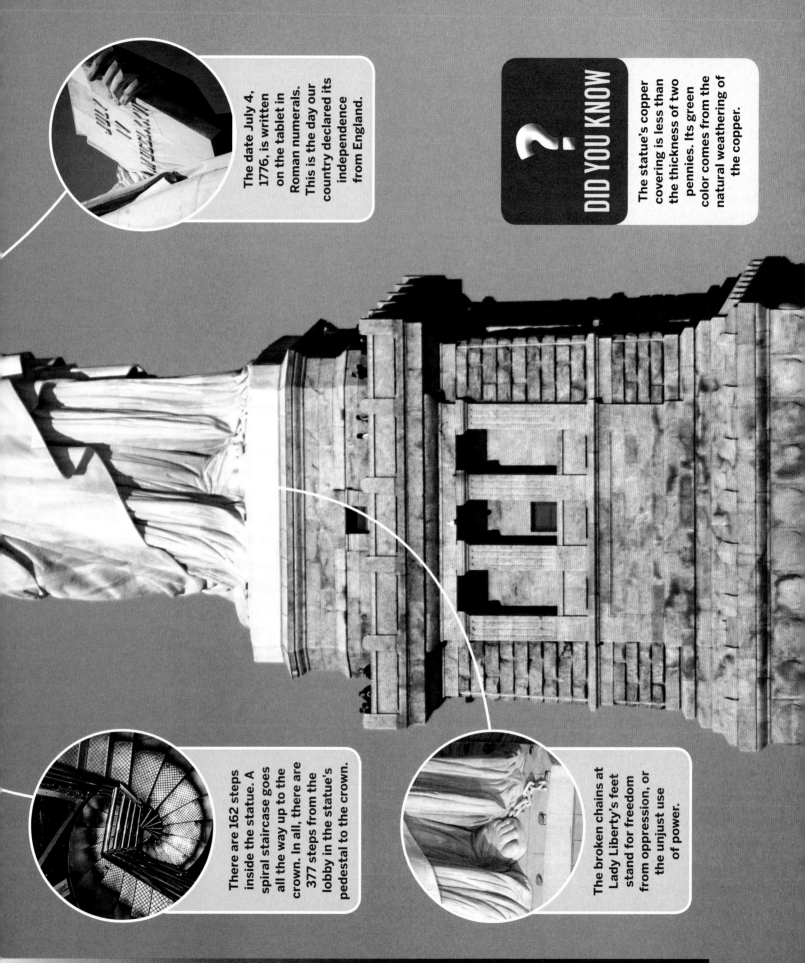

The date July 4, 1776, is written on the tablet in Roman numerals. This is the day our country declared its independence from England.

DID YOU KNOW

The statue's copper covering is less than the thickness of two pennies. Its green color comes from the natural weathering of the copper.

There are 162 steps inside the statue. A spiral staircase goes all the way up to the crown. In all, there are 377 steps from the statue's lobby in the statue's pedestal to the crown.

The broken chains at Lady Liberty's feet stand for freedom from oppression, or the unjust use of power.

Many People, One Country

There are many different kinds of people living in America. One thing they share: each person has an ethnicity. An ethnic group is made up of people who share the same culture, religion, or language. Imagine an American girl with one parent from Mexico and one from Germany. Both cultures are part of her ethnicity.

Why is America so ethnically diverse? When Europeans arrived in the 16th century, they brought with them African slaves. American Indians were already living on the continent. Some people living in the U.S. today are descendants of one of those groups. Most people living in the United States today are descendants of immigrants who have been coming from countries from all over the globe for hundreds of years. In the 1800s, immigrants to the United States came mostly from Europe. In the 1900s they started to arrive from other continents. Check out the bar graphs to learn more about how immigration has changed over the years.

WHERE DO IMMIGRANTS COME FROM?

Check out where most U.S. immigrants came from in 1960 compared with today:

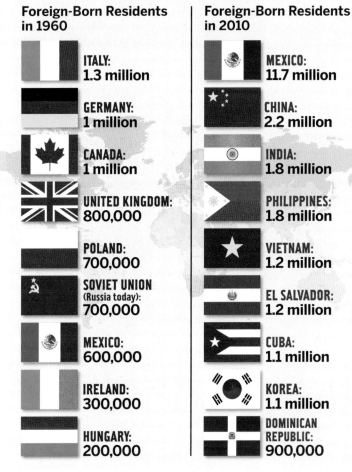

Foreign-Born Residents in 1960	Foreign-Born Residents in 2010
ITALY: 1.3 million	**MEXICO:** 11.7 million
GERMANY: 1 million	**CHINA:** 2.2 million
CANADA: 1 million	**INDIA:** 1.8 million
UNITED KINGDOM: 800,000	**PHILIPPINES:** 1.8 million
POLAND: 700,000	**VIETNAM:** 1.2 million
SOVIET UNION (Russia today): 700,000	**EL SALVADOR:** 1.2 million
MEXICO: 600,000	**CUBA:** 1.1 million
IRELAND: 300,000	**KOREA:** 1.1 million
HUNGARY: 200,000	**DOMINICAN REPUBLIC:** 900,000

Foreign-Born Population in the United States

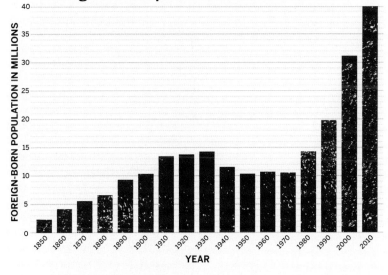

Chart information: U.S. Census Bureau (2010 survey)

Notable U.S. Immigrants

People from far and wide have traveled to the United States in search of a better life. Meet a few of the noteworthy immigrants who have arrived on our shores.

Name: Lupita Nyong'o
Born: March 1, 1983
Place of Origin: Mexico City, Mexico
Home in U.S.: Brooklyn, New York
Claim to Fame: The actress was born in Mexico, but raised in Kenya, Africa. In 2014, she won the Oscar for best supporting actress for her role in the movie *12 Years a Slave*.

Name: Indra Nooyi
Born: October 28, 1955
Place of Origin: Chennai, India
Home in U.S.: Greenwich, Connecticut
Claim to Fame: As the head of PepsiCo, she has pledged to move the company in a healthier direction. She pushed the company to remove unhealthy trans fats from its products.

Name: Dikembe Mutombo
Born: June 25, 1966
Place of Origin: Kinshasa, Democratic Republic of the Congo
Home in U.S.: Atlanta, Georgia
Claim to Fame: Off the court, the NBA great is known for his humanitarian work. His foundation has built hospitals and provided healthcare in his native Congo.

Name: Albert Einstein
Born: March 14, 1879
Place of Origin: Ulm, Germany
Home in U.S.: Princeton, New Jersey
Claim to Fame: He produced the famous math equation $E=mc^2$, which shows even a small amount of matter contains a lot of potential energy. The equation comes from Einstein's theory of relativity. He won the Nobel Prize in Physics in 1921.

Name: Ieoh Ming Pei
Born: April 26, 1917
Place of Origin: Guangzhou, China
Home in U.S.: Katonah, New York
Claim to Fame: The award-winning architect built the Rock and Roll Hall of Fame in Cleveland, Ohio (above). He also designed the glass pyramid that now stands at the entrance to the Louvre Museum in Paris, France.

Name: Madeleine Albright
Born: May 15, 1937
Place of Origin: Prague, Czechoslovakia (Czech Republic today)
Home in U.S.: Georgetown in Washington, DC
Claim to Fame: She was the first woman to become the U.S. secretary of state. President Bill Clinton nominated her and she was confirmed by a Senate vote of 99-0. She held the office from 1997 to 2001.

Name: Sergey Brin
Born: August 21, 1973
Place of Origin: Moscow, Soviet Union (Russia today)
Home in U.S.: Los Altos, California
Claim to Fame: He is a billionaire inventor, engineer, and computer programmer. He created the popular Google search engine with Stanford University classmate Larry Page in 1998.

Name: Isabel Allende
Born: August 2, 1942
Place of Origin: Lima, Peru
Home in U.S.: San Rafael, California
Claim to Fame: The author's first novel, *The House of the Spirits*, became a worldwide bestseller. President Barack Obama awarded her the Presidential Medal of Freedom in 2014. Although she was born in Peru, she is Chilean.

Name: Alexander Graham Bell
Born: March 3, 1847
Place of Origin: Edinburgh, Scotland
Home in U.S.: Cambridge, Massachusetts
Claim to Fame: He developed the first practical telephone. The Bell Telephone Company sprang up in 1877. Upon his death in 1922, the telephone system was shut down for one hour to honor him.

Name: Enrico Fermi
Born: September 29, 1901
Place of Origin: Rome, Italy
Home in U.S.: Chicago, Illinois
Claim to Fame: In 1938, he won the Nobel Prize for his work on radioactivity. As a leader on the Manhattan Project, he helped to develop the atomic bomb. The Enrico Fermi Award of the U.S. Department of Energy is given in his honor.

Soda or Pop?

You shouldn't drink too much of it. But if you want a little brown, bubbly cola, what do you call it? Soda? Pop? Coke? Think about what you call your grandparents. It might be mema and papa or nana and pops. Americans often use different words to refer to the same things. The words we use depend on where in the country we live. Here are some examples of words people have used in different parts of America in the past.

Wisconsin:
pop
New Jersey:
soda
Georgia:
soda pop
Alabama:
Coke
Tennessee:
cold drink

Louisiana: bayou
Massachusetts: brook
Illinois: creek
Florida: crick
Pennsylvania: run

South Carolina: battercake
Kentucky: flitter
California: hot cake
New York: flapjack
Michigan: griddle cake

Connecticut: grinder
Texas: poor boy
Pennsylvania: hoagie
Minnesota: torpedo sandwich
California: hero

Alabama: earthworm
Georgia: Georgia wiggler
Indiana: night crawler
North Dakota: angleworm
Virginia: bloodworm

Missouri: dragonfly
New Hampshire: devil's darning needle
Texas: mosquito hawk
Ohio: snake feeder
Minnesota: darning needle

Georgia: goober
South Carolina: ground nut
Alabama: ground pea
Illinois: goober pea
Florida: pinder

California: baby buggy
Maine: baby carriage
Michigan: baby cab
Pennsylvania: baby coach
Nebraska: stroller

California: long john
Maryland: long drawers
Oklahoma: long handles
Ohio: longies
New Jersey: long jeans

Georgia: big daddy
Tennessee: grandaddy
Alabama: pa
Rhode Island: papa
New Jersey: pop-pop

Chapter 7

MOMENTS THAT CHANGED AMERICA

The first moon landing represents just one of the many major events in history that shaped our country. In 1969, Neil Armstrong (shown here) became the first human to step foot on the moon. Turn the page to discover more of America's biggest defining moments.

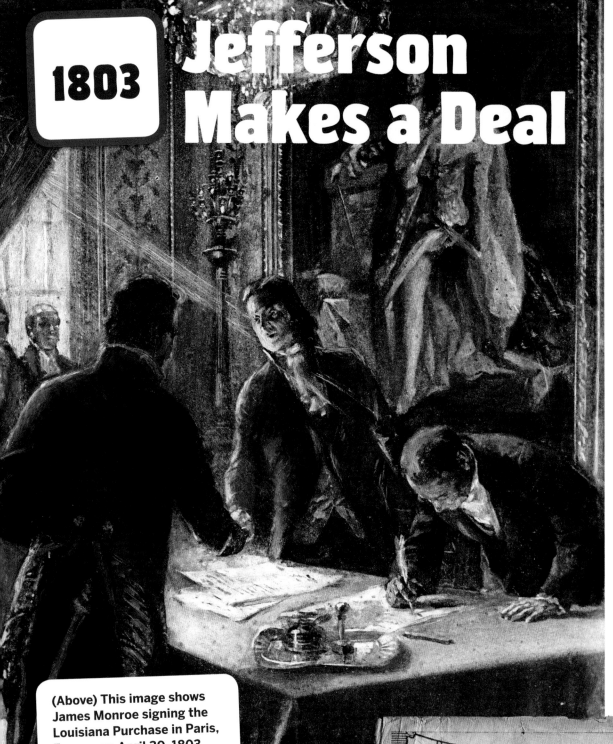

1803 Jefferson Makes a Deal

I n 1803, the third president of the United States made a really good decision. Thomas Jefferson bought from France 828,000 square miles of land known as the Louisiana Territory. The territory stretched from the Mississippi River in the east to the Rocky Mountains in the west (see map).

The deal, known as the Louisiana Purchase, nearly doubled the size of the country. The land was a bargain. Jefferson only paid a few pennies for each acre.

Immediately following the purchase, Americans began to expand westward into new lands. On April 30, 1812, Louisiana became the 18th state admitted to the United States. The Louisiana Territory would eventually be broken up to form 14 additional states.

(Above) This image shows James Monroe signing the Louisiana Purchase in Paris, France, on April 30, 1803. Monroe helped Thomas Jefferson to strike the land deal with France.

(Right) The U.S. map shows the land that makes up the Louisiana Purchase.

A Carpenter Strikes Gold

1848

On January 24, 1848, a carpenter named James Marshall was building a sawmill on the American River near Coloma, in northern California. He saw shiny flecks in the water. They were gold nuggets! So began the California Gold Rush.

Thousands of people rushed to the California territory. Men came from all over the world, ready to find their fortunes. These gold-miners became known as the '49ers because many of them arrived in 1849. About 250,000 had shown up by 1853—more people than live in the whole city of Orlando, Florida, today.

Little towns ballooned into big cities full of diverse people. Before 1848, California's population was 34,000. By 1860, the population was 380,000. The Gold Rush helped California become America's 31st state in 1850.

The Best Chance Yet, for CALIFORNIA!

A Meeting will be held in COHASSET, at the Office of

H. J. TURNER,

On SATURDAY, January 27th, at 11 O'Clock, for the purpose of forming a Company, to be called the "South Shore and California Joint Stock Company;" to be composed of 30 Members, and each Member paying $300.

COHASSET, JANUARY 24, 1849.

Propeller Power Presses, 142 Washington St., Boston.

(Left) James Marshall stands in front of Sutter's Mill in Coloma, California, where he discovered gold in 1848.

(Above) This ad from 1849 offers gold seekers travel from Boston, Massachusetts, to California.

1863

Lincoln Gives a Speech

O n November 19, 1863, Abraham Lincoln stood before a crowd of 15,000 people. He was dedicating a new cemetery in Gettysburg, Pennsylvania. His speech, which took three minutes to deliver, would become a key moment in U.S. history.

The U.S. was in the middle of a civil war. Eleven Southern states had seceded to form a new nation called the Confederate States of America, where slavery would continue to exist. Lincoln was determined to hold the Union together and end slavery.

The cemetery was for the Union soldiers who had died in the Battle of Gettysburg in July of 1863.

Lincoln described the Civil War as a test of whether the nation could survive. He said Americans had to keep fighting for the cause for which so many soldiers had given their lives. "Government of the people, by the people, for the people, shall not perish from the earth."

BY THE NUMBERS

In the first line of Lincoln's speech, he says that the Founding Fathers created America "four score and seven years ago."

—

A score = 20.

So four score = 4 x 20, or 80 years.

Four score and seven = 4 x 20 + 7, or 87 years

Lincoln gave his speech: 1863, 87 years after the Founding Fathers declared independence from Britain in 1776.

1869 A Railroad Goes From Coast to Coast

When gold miners rushed to California in 1849, they only had two transportation options: take a dangerous trip across land in a covered wagon or take a long, treacherous journey by sea. Either way, traveling across the U.S. could take four months and cost $1,000. That changed in 1869, when the first transcontinental railroad running from the Atlantic to the Pacific was completed. The trip took less than a week and cost just $150.

Two competing companies, the Central Pacific Railroad and the Union Pacific Railroad, raced to build the tracks. The Central Pacific Railroad Company began building the tracks in Sacramento, California, and the Union Pacific Railroad began work in Council Bluffs, Iowa.

After six years of hard work, the two groups of workers met in Promontory, Utah, on May 10, 1869. The final golden spike was driven into the ground, joining the two railroads.

One day later, the first transcontinental freight train chugged out of California heading east. On May 15, passenger service began.

THE GOLDEN SPIKE

The famous golden spike that finished the railroad was about 5 ½ inches long, and made from 4 ounces of gold worth $400. On one side, an inscription reads, "May God continue the unity of our country as this railroad unites the two great oceans of the world." On the top are three words: "The Last Spike."

1917 The United States Goes to War

O n April 6, 1917, the United States
entered World War I. The U.S. joined
the Allies, including Britain, France,
and Russia, to fight against the
Central Powers of Germany, Austria-
Hungary, Bulgaria, and Turkey.

When the war started in 1914, the U.S.
wished to remain neutral. The European
countries were fighting over territory and
other issues that did not concern Americans.
But events during the war changed those
feelings.

In May of 1915, a German submarine sank
the British passenger ship *Lusitania*. More
than 1,100 passengers died, among them 128

Americans. Then, in January 1917, the British
intercepted and decoded a secret telegram
sent from Germany to Mexico. The Germans
were offering Mexico territory in the U.S. if
Mexico would join Germany in the war.

President Woodrow Wilson had to act. He
asked Congress to declare war on Germany.
He said the U.S would go to war to "fight for
the ultimate peace of the world and for the
liberation of its peoples."

The U.S. troops arrived just in time. The
Allies were exhausted and running out of
soldiers. The entrance of 2 million U.S. troops
into the war helped to rally the Allies and to
defeat the Germans on November 11, 1918.

America Drops a Bomb

Germany became an enemy of the U.S. again in World War II, when it attacked others in Europe and murdered millions of Jewish people. One of Germany's allies was Japan, which attacked the U.S. in 1941.

On August 6, 1945, an American bomber plane dropped an atomic bomb on Hiroshima, Japan. About 80,000 people were killed in an instant. Three days later, another bomb was dropped on the city of Nagasaki, killing 40,000.

The bombs put a speedy end to World War II, but more than 50 million people had already died.

Many have wondered whether the invention of the atomic bomb was a mistake. By 1949, the Soviet Union (Russia today) had developed its own atomic bomb. The nuclear arms race had begun.

EINSTEIN'S ROLE

Scientist Albert Einstein is often incorrectly linked to the invention of nuclear weapons. His famous equation $E=mc^2$ explains the energy released in an atomic bomb. But the equation does not explain how to build one.

$E = mc^2$

A Long, Hard Trip to School

(Top) Soldiers stand ready to protect the Little Rock Nine outside of Central High School in Little Rock, Arkansas.

(Below) A white student berates Elizabeth Eckford, one of the first black students to be admitted to Little Rock Central High School, in Arkansas, on September 4, 1957.

In September of 1957, nine black students walked up the steps of Central High School in Little Rock, Arkansas. More than 1,000 armed U.S. soldiers stood by to protect them from angry white mobs. The Little Rock Nine, as they became known, were the first black students to enroll at the school.

In 1954, the U.S. Supreme Court had ruled that black and white students could no longer be forced to attend separate, or segregated, schools. The decision, *Brown v. Board of Education*, made school segregation illegal nationwide.

Why all the fury? Many people opposed the integration of schools because they believed races should not mix. Arkansas's governor, Orval Faubus, was one of them. He ordered the Arkansas National Guard to stop the Nine from entering the school. After a few weeks, President Dwight D. Eisenhower sent 1,000 armed soldiers to the scene. It took several tries, but the Little Rock Nine finally attended a full day of classes at Central High on September 25, 1957.

Little Rock's public schools did not become fully integrated until 1972. Now, racial discrimination is illegal in all areas, not just in schools.

Mankind Takes a Giant Leap

1969

I n the 1950s and 1960s, the U.S. and the Soviet Union (Russia today) raced to get to the moon first. Unmanned Soviet rockets landed on the moon, but the U.S. Apollo program put the first human on the moon.

On July 20, 1969, millions of Americans huddled around their TV sets to share in the historic moment of man's first steps on the moon. As he left the

spaceship, astronaut Neil Armstrong said these famous words: "That's one small step for man, one giant leap for mankind."

For 19 minutes, Armstrong stood alone where no human had ever stood before. Then crew member Edwin "Buzz" Aldrin joined him on the gray, dusty soil.

People had thought going to the moon was a plot for science fiction writers. On this day, it became American history.

BY THE NUMBERS

12
Number of astronauts who have walked on the moon

102
Number of hours it took the Apollo 11 astronauts to reach the moon

250°F
Temperature on the surface of the moon when the sun is shining on it.

842
Pounds of moon rocks and soil that Apollo astronauts brought back to Earth.

1989 The World Goes Online

EXCHANGING WORDS

Take a look at the way people have communicated throughout America's history.

1844: Samuel Morse sends the first message by telegraph, which allows people to communicate over long distances using a code of dashes and dots.

1860: Mail carriers known as the Pony Express take letters across the country.

1876: Alexander Graham Bell makes the first phone call.

1920s: Radios become common household items.

1973: Motorola makes the first handheld mobile phone.

The Internet was developed over many years by scientists and engineers. A big turning point was the invention in 1989 of the World Wide Web, which gave everyone access to an information system that had mostly been used by academics and government officials.

Today, rather than wait two weeks for a letter to get to India from Boston, anyone can send an email in an instant—and get one back in another! Ideas can be shared faster and more freely. In the click of a mouse, people in America can follow events happening in other parts of the world. Thanks to the Web, the entire planet has become more connected.

FUN FACT
About 87% of American adults use the Internet, according to a 2014 survey. Most of those Americans think the web is a pretty handy tool that has strengthened their personal relationships.

2001 A Tragic Attack

On September 11, terrorists hijacked four U.S. airplanes. They crashed two of them into New York City's World Trade Center, also known as the twin towers, where thousands of people were working. They crashed one plane into the Pentagon, the headquarters for the U.S. military just outside of Washington, D.C. The fourth plane crashed in the fields of Pennsylvania after the crew and passengers fought back against the hijackers. More than 3,000 Americans died on this day.

The moments that change America are often bright, happy achievements. But sometimes the moments that change America are dreadful events. The dark acts of these terrorists changed Americans' view of the world. After the attacks, the military began a worldwide search to find terrorists and stop them. This was the start of the war on terror.

Chapter 8

CIVIL RIGHTS

Americans are born with rights. They have the right to live in the city of their choice. They have the right to own land. They have the right to speak their minds. When each American turns 18, he or she gets the right to vote. All these privileges are known as civil rights.

The American government hasn't always been fair. Men and women didn't always have the same rights. People were treated unfairly based on the color of their skin. Many heroes in our country's history have worked to achieve equal rights for all Americans, no matter who they are or what they look like. These heroes have helped prove an important lesson. Sometimes being a great country means admitting you've been wrong and changing your ways.

Martin Luther King, Jr. gave his I Have a Dream speech at the Lincoln Memorial in Washington, D.C., on August 28, 1963.

An End to Slavery

Over the years, many states in the North banned slavery. But states in the South depended on slaves to produce their crops and make a living. They weren't ready to give up their way of life and let slaves go free.

Northerners and Southerners disagreed about many things, especially slavery. By 1861, many states in the South had tried to secede, or break away, from the U.S. and form their own country. The North, led by President Abraham Lincoln, wanted to keep the country in one piece. This dispute between the North and the South led to the Civil War.

The nation was divided. The battles were fierce. Many died. During the chaos, Lincoln made one of the most important announcements in America's history. On January 1, 1863, he declared that all slaves should be "forever free." He signed the Emancipation Proclamation. The document freed slaves in seceding states and inspired 179,000 slaves to join the Northern army to fight for freedom.

In 1865 the Civil War ended in a Northern victory. Congress passed the 13th amendment to the U.S. Constitution on December 6 of that year, forever outlawing slavery in every state in the nation.

This painting from 1862 shows President Abraham Lincoln reading the Emancipation Proclamation to his Cabinet.

Many African Americans living in the U.S. today are descended from slaves who fought for their own freedom in the Civil War. One out of every ten soldiers fighting for the North was black.

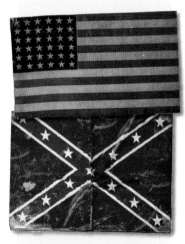

During the Civil War, Union soldiers from the North carried a flag with 36 stars, one for each state in the North and South. The flag of the Confederacy in the South had only 13 stars, one for each state on the Confederate side.

The Civil Rights Movement

The March on Washington in 1963 brought 250,000 to the National Mall in Washington, D.C.

One hundred years after the Civil War, black Americans led another fight for equality. The Civil War had ended slavery, but many people in the South still treated black people as lesser citizens. In some places, white and black people had to use separate restrooms and go to separate schools. White people got to sit in the front of buses, while black people had to sit in the back.

In the 1950s and 1960s, many Americans started to protest this treatment of people based on the color of their skin. In 1955, Rosa Parks refused to give up her bus seat for a white person. In 1960, four African-American college students in Greensboro, North Carolina, sat at a lunch counter reserved for white people and politely refused to leave until they were served. In 1961, white people who supported civil rights for all joined black people, led by John Lewis, on "freedom rides" through the South to protest segregated transportation. Each one of these events inspired many others.

MARCHING ON WASHINGTON

The best-known leader of the Civil Rights Movement was Reverend Martin Luther King, Jr. In 1963, King stood on the steps of the Lincoln Memorial before 250,000 people who had marched through the streets of Washington, D.C. They had gathered to protest the unfair treatment of black Americans. "I have a dream," King told them, "that one day this nation will rise up and live out the true meaning of its creed: 'We hold these truths to be self-evident, that all men are created equal.'"

A LONG ROAD

Here are some highlights of the Civil Rights Movement. This time of change lasted from 1954 to 1965.

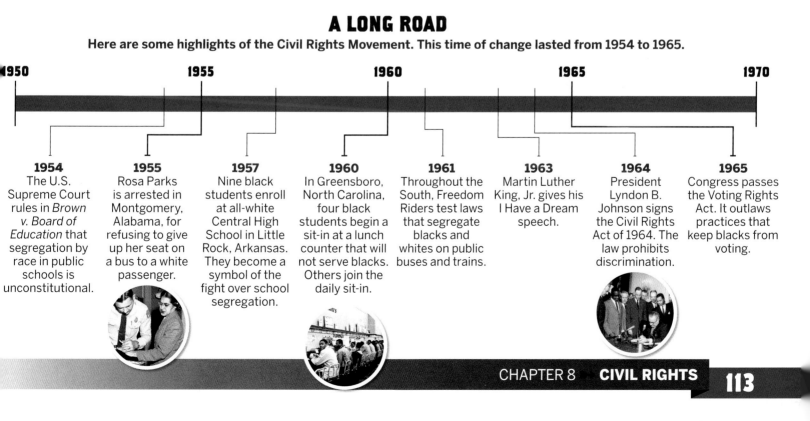

1950   **1955**   **1960**   **1965**   **1970**

1954
The U.S. Supreme Court rules in *Brown v. Board of Education* that segregation by race in public schools is unconstitutional.

1955
Rosa Parks is arrested in Montgomery, Alabama, for refusing to give up her seat on a bus to a white passenger.

1957
Nine black students enroll at all-white Central High School in Little Rock, Arkansas. They become a symbol of the fight over school segregation.

1960
In Greensboro, North Carolina, four black students begin a sit-in at a lunch counter that will not serve blacks. Others join the daily sit-in.

1961
Throughout the South, Freedom Riders test laws that segregate blacks and whites on public buses and trains.

1963
Martin Luther King, Jr. gives his I Have a Dream speech.

1964
President Lyndon B. Johnson signs the Civil Rights Act of 1964. The law prohibits discrimination.

1965
Congress passes the Voting Rights Act. It outlaws practices that keep blacks from voting.

Battles Over Indian Lands

American Indians had been living in America for hundreds of years before the first European colonists arrived in the 1600s. Sometimes, the Indians and the colonists built friendships and helped each other.

But many times American Indians were treated cruelly or killed by white people.

In the 1800s, the American military battled Indian tribes. Defeated tribes had to give up lands in the East in exchange for lands in the unsettled West.

Some Indians stood their ground. President Andrew Jackson sent in the military. The Indians were forced to give up their homes and march west. By the end of the 1830s, almost 50,000 Indians had been removed from their lands in the East.

This painting depicts the removal of Cherokee Indians to the West In 1838. This event is known as the Trail of Tears.

1924	1956	567	5 million
American Indians are made U.S. citizens	American Indians win the right to vote everywhere in the U.S.	The number of different American Indian tribes in the U.S.	The number of American Indians in the U.S. today

On November 9, 1969, a group of American Indians took a boat to the island of Alcatraz in the San Francisco Bay in California. The island was home to America's most infamous prison, but it had been shut down. The American Indians claimed the island for Indian tribes. They stayed there for almost two years before the FBI removed them. While they controlled the island, they chanted: "We hold the rock."

As America expanded west, settlers again took the land that had been given to American Indians. Years later, our government tried to make up for these injustices. Today, hundreds of tribes live on reservations.

The Fight for Latino Rights

People of Hispanic or Latino descent make up the nation's biggest ethnic minority. As of 2015, about one out of every five people in the United States says he or she is Hispanic or Latino. These are people of Cuban, Mexican, Puerto Rican, South American, Central American, or other Spanish or Latin-American culture.

Many of their battles for civil rights have been fought on America's richest farmland. Immigrants have long found work in the fields of states like California. Landowners have often treated these workers unfairly—making them work long, sweaty days for a tiny wage. In 1903, about 1,200 Latino and Japanese immigrants organized the first farm workers'

union. A union is an association of workers that demands rights as a group. Banding together, people have more power than working on their own.

Before the Civil Rights Act of 1964 made segregation illegal, many Hispanic and Latino children suffered the same unequal treatment as African Americans, such as attending segregated

In 1975, thousands of protesters join the United Farm Workers' 1,000-mile march in California to call attention to workers' rights.

THE GRAPE BOYCOTT

Like Martin Luther King, Jr., civil rights activist Cesar Chavez believed in protesting without violence. In 1965, immigrant workers from grape farms decided to go on strike. That means they refused to go to work until their bosses treated them better. The grape workers asked Chavez to strike with them. He did more than that. Chavez helped convince people across the U.S. not to eat any California grapes. If the farm owners couldn't sell their crops, they would have to listen to the strikers' demands. Millions of people stopped buying grapes in grocery stores and eating them in desserts. The farm owners eventually backed down, agreeing to give workers better pay and treatment.

schools. Even recently, children and adults who speak Spanish have been denied opportunities that English-speakers get. Civil rights leaders have demanded equal treatment and respect for Hispanic and Latino cultures. "Preservation of one's own culture does not require contempt or disrespect for other cultures," said union leader Cesar Chavez.

Dolores Huerta

HARVESTING HOPE

Dolores Huerta is a labor leader who, like Cesar Chavez, fought for the rights of farm workers. She started the Agricultural Workers Association in 1960. She then co-founded with Chavez in 1962 the workers' union that came to be known as United Farm Workers. To this day, she continues to work to better the lives of workers, immigrants, and children.

GREAT AMERICANS

"I have not failed. I've just found 10,000 ways that won't work."
— Thomas Edison, inventor of the lightbulb

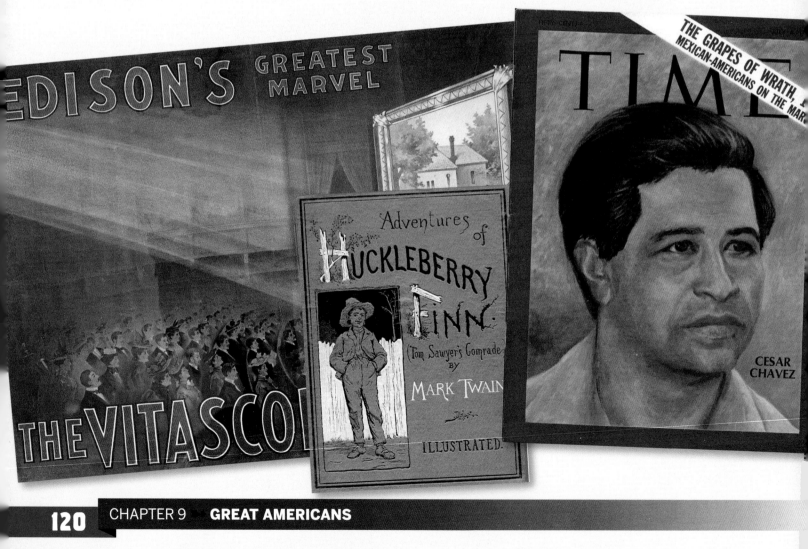

ROBINSON 3b-of BROOKLYN DODGERS

GEORGE HERMAN (BABE) RUTH

BIG LEAGUE CHEWING GUM

THE SPHERE
The Empire's Illustrated Weekly   London, May 28, 1932

FITZGERALD
HALLELUJAH

America is a young country compared to nations in Europe and Asia. It's a place where people seek new ideas and new experiences. Many great Americans are people who tried something no one else had tried before. And when some of them failed, these men and women tried and tried again! From athletes to inventors to painters, here are some people who have done America proud.

Thomas Edison
INVENTOR | 1847-1931

Edison's genius launched the electrical revolution. The list of his inventions goes on and on. But one of his greatest accomplishments was the system of invention that he helped pioneer.

In the 1870s, at Menlo Park, Edison created an "invention factory." He brought together a team of scientists and engineers to develop all kinds of inventions, big and small. Today, companies such as Ford and Google follow his example.

Edison holds 1,093 U.S. patents for his inventions. Here are a few.

1877
Edison built a device called the *phonograph* that could capture sounds and play them back. The first words he recorded were, "Mary had a little lamb."

1879
There were some electric lights around before Edison invented his famous *bulb*. But his invention was the first light that was cheap enough for people to use in their homes.

1892
Edison invented a movie camera called the *kinetograph*. The camera allowed people to see moving pictures for the first time ever.

Samuel Morse
INVENTOR | 1791-1872

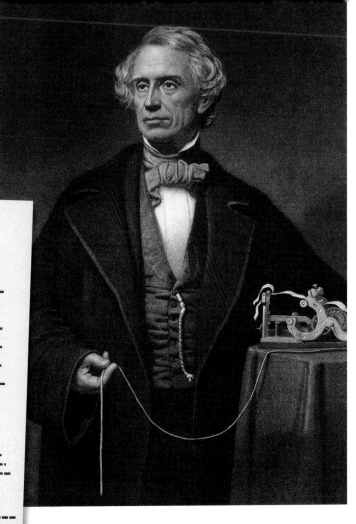

I n 1840, before there were telephones, Samuel Morse invented the telegraph machine, which sent electrical signals over long distances through wires. Morse used a code of dots and dashes to represent letters and numbers (see "Get the Message").

Using Morse code, people could report news from across the country and send important messages in a jiffy.

GET THE MESSAGE
The chart shows the alphabet in Morse code.

MORSE ALPHABET.
(INTERNATIONAL MORSE.)

Letters.

Numbers.

Stops and Signs.

Alexander Graham Bell
INVENTOR | 1847-1922

S amuel Morse's discovery helped Alexander Graham Bell come up with another invention that changed the world: the telephone. Instead of transmitting dots and dashes, as in Morse code, Bell's telephone was built to send human voices through a wire. In 1876, Bell used the device for the first time, calling his assistant from the next room. "Mr. Watson," he said. "Come here. I want to see you." These were the first words ever spoken over the telephone!

Charles Lindbergh
PILOT | 1902–1974

Charles Lindbergh made a wild journey across the Atlantic in 1927. The 25-year-old pilot took off from Long Island in New York. He was headed for Paris. Many doubted he would make it. Others had attempted the same journey and failed. When he landed 33 hours later, Lindbergh became the first person to make a nonstop flight across the Atlantic Ocean on his own. He had flown 3,500 miles!

Thousands of people had been waiting to find out if he would land safely. "There has never been an adventure into the air into which was packed so much daring, skill, and romance as this feat of Lindbergh's," wrote the *New York Times*.

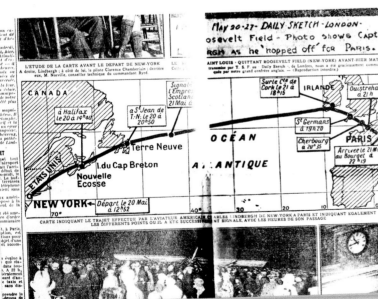

WHAT A TRIP!

The front page of this Paris newspaper shows Charles Lindbergh arriving in France after his record-breaking flight across the Atlantic Ocean in 1927. Here are a few fun facts about the trip.

- Lindbergh took four sandwiches with him.

- His plane, the *Spirit of St. Louis*, held 451 gallons of gas.

- One of Lindbergh's biggest challenges on the flight was staying awake. Between preparations and the journey itself, he went some 55 hours without sleep.

Amelia Earhart
PILOT | 1897-1937

Amelia Earhart broke all kinds of records, proving to the world that women are just as daring as men. First, she flew a plane higher than any woman had before. Then she flew planes farther and faster than had any other woman in the world.

In 1932, she became the first woman to fly solo across the Atlantic Ocean. The trip took 15 hours.

Sadly, Earhart did not succeed in her last adventure. In 1937, she set out to fly around the world. When she tried to land on a tiny island in the Pacific, her plane disappeared. The U.S. Navy searched for Earhart and her one passenger, navigator Frederick J. Noonan. They were never found. Today, people are still looking for the plane, which is likely somewhere at the bottom of the ocean.

Babe Ruth
ATHLETE | 1895-1948

Babe Ruth was such a good baseball player that one of his teammates said he "wasn't human." He was like a superhero who could hit home run after home run. The New York Yankee played his greatest season in 1927 when he hit 60 home runs, a record that remained unbroken until 1961.

In 1932, the Yankees were playing a tough game against the Chicago Cubs. Ruth stepped up to bat and swung twice. He missed both times. Then he pointed his finger. Later, he said he was "calling his shot," pointing to show where he was going to hit the ball. He hit a home run and it became a legendary moment in baseball history.

Jackie Robinson
ATHLETE | 1919-1972

Back in the days when black and white Americans ate at separate lunch counters and used different water fountains, they also played on separate sports teams. That changed in 1947, when baseball great Jackie Robinson became the first African American to play

BEYOND BASEBALL

Meet some of America's other record-breaking athletes.

MICHAEL JORDAN, born 1963:
The Chicago Bulls basketball player didn't make his varsity team in high school. But he kept at it and became a superstar. He won six basketball championships, and young people across America wanted to "Be Like Mike."

JACKIE JOYNER-KERSEE, born 1962:
Joyner-Kersee was a queen of track and field. She could jump hurdles, sprint, and throw the javelin. She won six Olympic medals and once completed a long jump that was more than 24 feet!

JOE MONTANA, born 1956:
Quarterback Joe Montana wasn't the biggest or strongest player. But he was smart and calm. The San Francisco 49er won four Super Bowls and he was named Most Valuable Player in three of those games.

MUHAMMAD ALI, born 1942:
Muhammad Ali was a boxer known as "The Greatest." He bragged about his ability to "float like a butterfly and sting like a bee." While Ali was a fighter in the boxing ring, he was against war. Ali refused to join the military because of his religious beliefs.

BILLIE JEAN KING, born 1943:
Billie Jean King was ranked for five years as the world's best female tennis player. When she wasn't winning Grand Slams, she was fighting for female athletes to be taken seriously. In a famous victory, in 1973, she beat a former male tennis champion.

in the major leagues. People said he broke the "color barrier."

Robinson had to deal with many unkind words from other players and fans. But he kept his cool and became one of the best players in the league.

Robinson made six trips to the World Series and helped inspire the Civil Rights Movement that would start a few years later.

Maya Angelou
POET | 1928-2014

Maya Angelou put words together the way a talented painter puts colors together with her brush.

Angelou wrote more than 30 books. She was also an actress and an advocate for civil rights. More than one president has asked her to read a poem in front of the country. Like Mark Twain, she proved that her pen could do big things.

Mark Twain
AUTHOR | 1835-1910

Mark Twain was a great American storyteller. He used humor to call attention to injustices in the world. In novels like *The Adventures of Tom Sawyer* (1876) and *The Adventures of Huckleberry Finn* (1885), Twain created classic characters while addressing issues such as racism and slavery.

"All modern American literature comes from one book by Mark Twain called *Huckleberry Finn*," author Ernest Hemingway famously declared in 1935. "It's the best book we've had. All American writing comes from that." Hemingway noted that in *Huckleberry Finn*, readers heard the voices of everyday people for the first time in American literature.

Today, *Huckleberry Finn* is required reading in many high schools and remains among the most taught works of American literature.

WHAT'S IN A NAME?

Mark Twain's real name was Samuel Clemens. He got his pen name from working on steamboats on the Mississippi River. When a member of the crew yelled "mark twain!" that meant the water in the river had been measured and it was deep enough for the boat to travel through.

1937: Snow White
1940: Pinocchio
1940: Fantasia
1941: Dumbo
1942: Bambi
1950: Cinderella
1951: Alice in Wonderland
1953: Peter Pan
1955: Lady and the Tramp
1959: Sleeping Beauty
1961: 101 Dalmatians
1963: The Sword in the Stone
1967: The Jungle Book
1973: Robin Hood
1977: The Rescuers
1977: The Many Adventures of Winnie the Pooh
1981: The Fox and the Hound
1986: The Great Mouse Detective
1989: The Little Mermaid
1991: Beauty and the Beast
1992: Aladdin
1994: The Lion King
1995: Pocahontas
1996: The Hunchback of Notre Dame
1997: Hercules
1998: Mulan
2002: Lilo & Stitch
2009: The Princess and the Frog
2010: Tangled
2013: Frozen

Walt Disney
ANIMATOR | 1901-1966

Walt Disney was a pioneer of animated films. He loved to draw as a boy, and when he grew up he became an artist in Kansas City. Later he moved to California and invented the popular cartoon character, Mickey Mouse. People loved Mickey, and so Disney created more characters, like Minnie Mouse and Donald Duck. Disney's company grew. In 1937, he made one of the world's first animated movies, *Snow White and the Seven Dwarves*. In 1955, he opened the theme park Disneyland in Anaheim, California, where people could visit the characters he had created.

Even though Walt Disney is no longer around, his company still makes movies and runs theme parks that millions of people around the world enjoy. The time line on the right highlights some of the stories Disney has told in the last century.

Louis Armstrong
MUSICIAN | 1901-1971

Jazz music was invented in America, and one of the most talented jazz musicians of all time was the trumpet player Louis Armstrong.

Armstrong was born in New Orleans, Louisiana. That southern city is also the birthplace of jazz. Armstrong grew up poor and sang on the streets to make a little money for his family. Soon he was traveling and playing in jazz bands all over the country. As jazz music became more popular around the world, so did he.

Armstrong became a worldwide star. He could blow his horn with more force than anyone else. Though he died in 1971, the music he made is still influencing musicians today.

ALL THAT JAZZ
Jazz is all about rhythm. Musicians get together on stage, and they improvise. That means they don't follow sheet music note by note, as a symphony does. They come up with their lively sounds and beats on the spot! Jazz musicians can take a song people have heard a hundred times and make it sound brand new.

Ella Fitzgerald
SINGER | 1917-1996

Like Louis Armstrong, Ella Fitzgerald had a hard life but made music that put a smile on people's faces. She was known as the "First Lady of Song" and was famous for singing swing. Swing is a fast-paced, hard-beating type of jazz. Fitzgerald sang other types of groovy jazz, as well as blues and classics. Her voice was rich and playful. She could sing low or high. In 1958, she became the first African-American woman to win a Grammy Award, America's highest honor for musicians. By the end of her life, Fitzgerald had won 14 Grammys and had become a national treasure.

George and Ira Gershwin

COMPOSERS | 1898–1937 (George)/ 1896–1983 (Ira)

The Gershwin brothers were a songwriting team from New York City. Their music was some of the most popular during the Jazz Age, and it is still played today. The Gershwins wrote for dozens of Broadway musicals and Hollywood films. They composed jazz, pop, opera, and romantic pieces on the piano.

Ira, the older brother, mostly came up with the words. George, a talented piano player, mostly came up with the melodies. Together, their tunes had people around the country dancing and singing.

Songwriters and singers can't do much without each other. America's top singers—including Ella Fitzgerald and Louis Armstrong—all played versions of the Gershwins' songs.

The brothers' legacy lives on in the Gershwin Room at the Library of Congress in Washington, D.C. Visitors can hear their music and even check out George's piano and Ira's typewriter.

A GREAT AMERICAN OPERA

The Gershwin brothers are credited with writing the first great American opera. *Porgy and Bess* premiered on Broadway in 1935. It was a common practice at the time to cast white actors to play the roles of African Americans. The Gershwins, however, insisted on hiring only black singers.

Since its Broadway debut more than 80 years ago, the portrayal of African-American life in the South has been performed all over the world. Many consider *Porgy and Bess* the Gershwins' crowning achievement.

Martin Luther King, Jr.

CIVIL RIGHTS ACTIVIST | 1929-1968

Martin Luther King, Jr., was a Baptist minister raised in Georgia who became a leader in the Civil Rights Movement. King might have done more than any other person to fight for equality for all races in America. He helped to end Jim Crow laws, which allowed separating people based on the color of their skin.

King knew words could move people, and as a minister he got a lot of practice stringing words together. King convinced thousands of people to peacefully protest against racism. His most famous speech is known as the I Have a Dream speech. Before the Lincoln Memorial in Washington, D.C., in 1963, he talked about his dream for America's future.

"I have a dream that my four little children will one day live in a nation where they will not be judged by the color of their skin but by the content of their character," King said. "I have a dream today!"

King won the Nobel Peace Prize in 1964, the same year President Lyndon Johnson signed a new law that ended Jim Crow. But the law was controversial. Many people didn't like it or the ideas King stood for. In 1968, King was shot and killed while standing on the balcony of a hotel in Memphis, Tennessee.

CORETTA SCOTT KING

King's wife was Coretta Scott King. She worked with him throughout their marriage, fighting for civil rights. It was her idea to establish a national holiday on her husband's birthday. Every year America celebrates King's life on Martin Luther King, Jr. Day, the third Monday in January.

Rosa Parks
CIVIL RIGHTS ACTIVIST | 1913-2005

In 1955, Rosa Parks refused to give up her seat on a segregated bus in Montgomery, Alabama. At the time, the seats in the front of the bus were reserved for white people.

When the bus driver demanded Parks get out of her seat in the "colored" section so a white man could sit down, she didn't budge. She was arrested.

Martin Luther King, Jr. used her story to convince black people in Montgomery to boycott the bus. After a year, the boycott worked. Buses in Montgomery never had sections for different races again.

Cesar Chavez
ACTIVIST | 1927-1993

So much food is grown in California that people call the state "the Salad Bowl of the World." Many of the workers who tend to those crops are Mexican-Americans or other immigrants.

In the 1930s, Cesar Chavez and his family were farm workers in America. He learned firsthand how hard the lives of migrant farm workers could be. Farm workers were feeding the country, and yet they received terrible pay and worked in rough conditions. Sometimes a whole family would only get a few dimes for hours of work.

Chavez decided to do something about it. He became a champion of farm workers and fought his entire life for them to be treated better.

One of Wright's most famous buildings is called Fallingwater (pictured below at left). It was built over a waterfall in Pennsylvania in 1935. This is the type of dramatic work that has inspired generations of architects who came after Wright. Take a look at some of the structures he created.

Frank Lloyd Wright Residence (interior)
Oak Park, Illinois
1889

Unitarian Church (exterior)
Shorewood Hills, Wisconsin
1951

Guggenheim Museum (interior)
New York, New York
1959

Frank Lloyd Wright
ARCHITECT | 1867-1959

Architect Frank Lloyd Wright didn't like fancy designs. Rather than making buildings with lots of decorations, he made buildings that fit into their natural surroundings. Many of the homes he built were long and open. He used windows to let in natural light and materials like wood to show the beauty of nature. Wright's fresh style was something people had never seen before. This style of architecture came to be known as "Prairie School."

Fallingwater (exterior)
Mill Run, Pennsylvania
1935

Series 1, No. 4

Georgia O'Keeffe
PAINTER | 1887–1986

Georgia O'Keeffe was a bold painter who created bright landscapes and abstract art. (Abstract art expresses an idea, but the images may not look like anything in the real world.) She painted animal skulls, skyscrapers, and flowers, but not in a traditional way. She looked at art from the past and decided to take her work in a new direction.

Maya Lin
ARTIST | BORN 1959

When Maya Lin was still in college, she won a national competition to design a monument honoring soldiers who died in the Vietnam War. Her design did not look like past war memorials. It was a polished, V-shaped, black granite wall. Inscribed in the wall are the names of the more than 58,000 soldiers who died in the war.

The Vietnam Memorial opened in 1982. It sits at the northwest corner of the National Mall, in Washington, D.C.

Chapter 10

GROWING UP IN AMERICA

America is called the land of opportunity. The following pages capture the experience of growing up, making a living, and having fun in this country.

The Big Years

Long ago, people measured the distance from place to place with rocks. After each mile, they'd leave a stone. If you walked past five stones, you knew you were five miles from where you started.

Today people call big moments in life milestones, because these events help us to measure how far we've come in life. Here are some milestones of growing up in America.

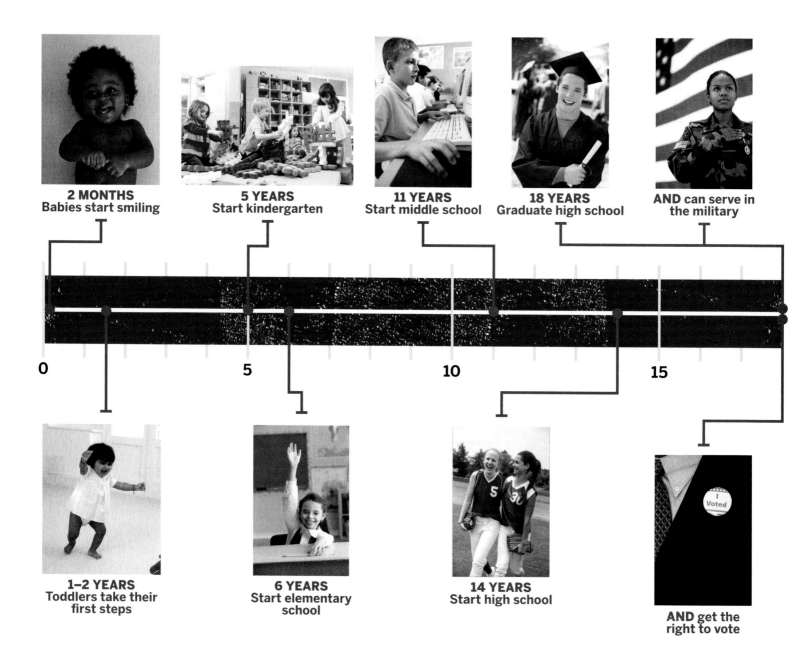

2 MONTHS
Babies start smiling

5 YEARS
Start kindergarten

11 YEARS
Start middle school

18 YEARS
Graduate high school

AND can serve in the military

0   5   10   15

1–2 YEARS
Toddlers take their first steps

6 YEARS
Start elementary school

14 YEARS
Start high school

AND get the right to vote

The American Dream

> "**W**e hold these truths to be self-evident, that all men are created equal, that they are endowed by their Creator with certain unalienable Rights, that among these are *Life, Liberty and the pursuit of Happiness.*"
> —**The Declaration of Independence**

Work hard and you will prosper. That's the "American Dream." From generation to generation, Americans hold on to the hope that a better, richer, and happier life is within reach for all, no matter who we are, where we live, or how wealthy our parents.

The American Dream means different things to different people. For some people, the American Dream is having a family and owning a home. For others, the American Dream is a college degree and a rewarding career. For yet others, the American Dream might be the freedom to define happiness for themselves.

The American Dream has been more difficult to achieve for some Americans than for others. But sometimes the hardest fights bring the sweetest victories.

Life in the 1700s

While some black workers in the North were free, slavery was still allowed in many parts of America. The country was built on the labor of black Americans in its early years.

People used trusty horses, wagons, and carriages to get around.

Sometimes a town's library would be kept in the home of a farmer, if his farmhouse was big enough.

The Residence of David Twining (1845), by Edward Hicks

There weren't many schools in the 1700s. Most parents taught their kids to read and write at home. About 25% of Americans never learned to read at all!

Many families lived on small farms near small towns. They made a living by fishing, growing crops, and blacksmithing (making and repairing iron items by hand).

Men wore fancy outfits with coats, hats, scarves, and sometimes wigs. They were in charge of running the family's property, even if a woman owned the land.

Nearly all Americans owned a Bible. About 80% of Americans attended church.

Life in the 1800s

In the 1800s, American cities were growing fast. Ships of immigrants arrived every day from countries around the world. Cities got so crowded that families had to live in small, rundown apartments.

Men were the "breadwinners." They worked to support their families.

Immigrants brought books, recipes, and traditions with them from their home countries.

Pre-sliced bread, like the kind you find in the grocery store today, didn't exist yet. People had to slice their own.

By the end of the 1800s, millions of children attended public elementary schools. At first, children ages 6 to 16 might be lumped together in one classroom. But in 1848, the educator Horace Mann introduced the idea of separating kids into different grades.

Just Moved (1870) by Henry Mosler

Many mothers made clothes for their families. Women almost never wore pants. They were expected to wear long, modest skirts and dresses.

There was a lot of work to do at home. Clothes had to be washed with buckets and washboards like this one.

Life in the 1900s

People started to move to places called suburbs on the edge of big cities. There, people could find more space and live in bigger homes.

Some women were homemakers, yet many women started to have careers outside the home. They proved they could be breadwinners just like men.

The invention of affordable automobiles changed life in America. Businesses could deliver goods to more customers. Many Americans went on long drives every Sunday just for fun.

When World War II ended, many couples decided they wanted to start families. This time became known as the "baby boom."

By 1918, every state had passed a law requiring kids to go to school. Many kids in the 1800s went only to elementary school. In the 1900s, the majority of kids for the first time attended high school.

Life in the 2000s

Stay-at-home dads are on the rise in the U.S. The number of fathers who stay at home with their children has nearly doubled, to 2 million, since 1989.

Nearly 70% of women with children under 18 years old work. America's working mothers are now the primary breadwinners in a record 40% of households, up from 11% in 1960.

Teens and older gamers spend about six hours each week playing video games.

On average, children ages 2 to 11 watch more than 24 hours of TV each week. Adults ages 35 to 49 watch more than 33 hours.

Today, American kids' free time is eaten up by screen time. Children often spend just minutes each day outdoors. There is a movement across the country to encourage kids to put down their iPads and head outside.

ELECTRIC VEHICLE CHARGING STATION

More Americans are investing in electric cars to save on gas and do their part for the environment.

What Makes Americans Happy?

M any scientists have tried to figure out the secrets to happiness. Here are some of the discoveries they've made about Americans and what makes them happy at different stages in their lives.

HAPPINESS THROUGH THE AGES

AS A KID
technology, toys, hobbies, playing team sports, having pets

11 years old
About half of American kids have their first mobile phone by this age

40%
Almost half of American households have a dog

8 students
Eight out of every 10 American students graduate from high school

62 million
Number of Americans who volunteer each year

220,000
Today, more than 200,000 kids live in a home with two dads or two moms, rather than one mom and one dad.

126 million
Number of Americans with passports

9 hours
Kids should get between 9 and 11 hours of sleep each night. Adults should get at least 7.

AS A TEENAGER
getting good grades, making best friends, having good relationships with parents

AS A YOUNG ADULT
volunteering, random acts of kindness, attending religious services, running, exercising

AS ADULTS
getting married, making money, having a job, yoga and meditation

AS OLDER ADULTS
having kids, eating healthy food (not being overweight), getting a good night's sleep, traveling

Chapter 11

AMERICA'S ROLE

We all need a little help from our friends. Countries are the same way. Any country that is friendly with America is known as an ally. Allies fight on the same side in a war, as in the Revolutionary War when France helped the colonies defeat Britain. Allies lend money to one another. They work together to solve problems, like protecting the environment. Sometimes they even give one another great presents, like the Statue of Liberty. (Thanks, France!)

Now that our country is all grown up, we're making our mark in the world. We are known for our military might, but also for our top-notch athletes and entertainers. Turn the page to learn more.

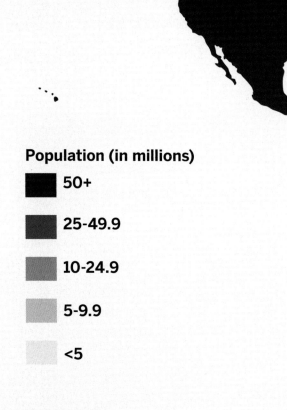

Population (in millions)

50+

25-49.9

10-24.9

5-9.9

<5

IN THE WORLD

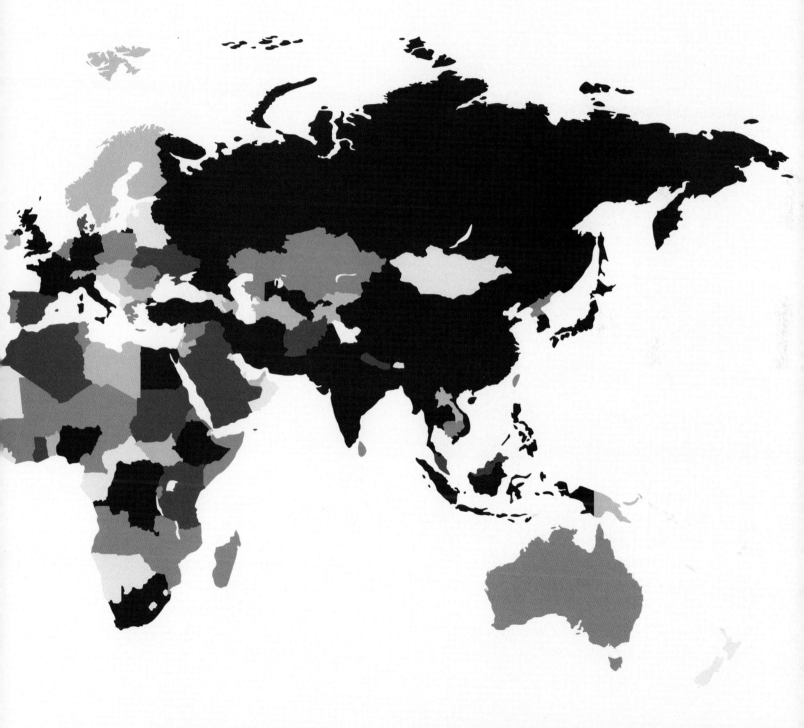

America's Military

On May 2, 2011, U.S. troops stormed this final hiding place of terrorist Osama bin Laden, in Abbottabad, Pakistan.

In the middle of the night on May 2, 2011, two helicopters landed in Pakistan. About two dozen armed U.S. troops jumped out of the copters and snuck into a compound with 18-foot walls. They believed one of America's greatest enemies was hiding inside.

The troops climbed up the stairs in the dark and fought off men who tried to attack them. They found the terrorist Osama bin Laden, the man responsible for 9/11 (see page 105), and the troops shot him. The mission was dangerous but successful, and the men who risked their lives became heroes.

This mission, carried out by Navy SEALs, is just one example of the work of the American military. Other men and women of the military patrol the sky and waters around America. Some fly fighter jets or break secret codes. Today, there are about 1.4 million people in the active U.S. armed forces. The president, known as the commander-in-chief, is the top dog of the U.S. military.

AIR FORCE

Members of the Air Force work to protect America in the air and in space. Their job is to fly planes, helicopters, and satellites. The Air Force was once part of the Army but became its own military branch in 1947. That makes it the youngest branch.

Established: 1947
Motto: "Aim High ... Fly-Fight-Win"
What they're called: Airmen and Airwomen

ARMY

The Army is the largest and oldest branch of the U.S. military. Its history dates back to the time of George Washington, who was the Army's top officer in the Revolutionary War. The Army soldier's job is to defend the country, especially in battles that take place on land.

Established: 1775
Motto: "This We'll Defend"
What they're called: Soldiers

COAST GUARD

The Coast Guard operates in waters around the U.S. In peacetime, the Coast Guard is like a police force that tracks down criminals on the ocean and performs rescue missions at sea. In war time, the president can send the Coast Guard to fight alongside the Navy.

Established: 1790
Motto: "Semper Paratus" (Latin for "Always Ready")
What they're called: Guardsmen and Guardswomen

MARINE CORPS

Marines are trained for missions that take place on sea and on land. They're known for being tough and quick. Often they'll be the first troops who are sent to fight in a conflict overseas. The Marine Corps is the second smallest branch, after the Coast Guard.

Established: 1775
Motto: "Semper Fidelis" (Latin for "Always Faithful")
What they're called: Marines

NAVY

The Navy's main job is to defend freedom on the water. The Navy also conducts missions on the land and in the air. A Navy SEAL is an elite fighter in the armed forces. The name SEAL stands for SEa, Air, and Land.

Established: 1775
Motto: "Semper Fortis" (Latin for "Always Brave")
What they're called: Sailors

The Peace Corps

(Top) A Peace Corps volunteer teaches an adult education class in Honduras. (Inset) President John F. Kennedy greets Peace Corps volunteers.

I n a speech at the University of Michigan in 1960, John F. Kennedy challenged students to spend two years of their lives helping people in less fortunate nations around the world. As president, Kennedy turned that idea into the Peace Corps, a volunteer organization promoting peace and friendship around the world. Thousands of people signed up in the first few months. They went off to Ghana, in Africa, to serve as teachers. Five decades later, Peace Corps volunteers have traveled to more than 40 countries, trying to understand the ways of life in those countries and help those countries to understand Americans.

PEACEFUL PROJECTS

Check out some of the Peace Corps missions.

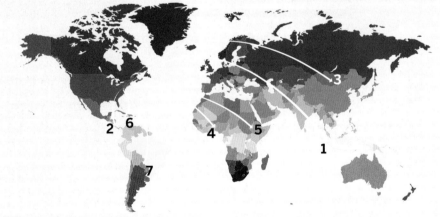

1. **Indonesia:** Helping people find housing and food after a deadly tsunami
2. **Costa Rica:** Teaching young girls ballet to help them build self-confidence
3. **Mongolia:** Working to organize the country's first Special Olympics
4. **Benin:** Fighting malaria, a deadly disease spread by mosquitos
5. **Ethiopia:** Running from town to town to teach people about the disease HIV
6. **Haiti:** Growing vegetable gardens to help local farmers
7. **Paraguay:** Leading cooking classes to help people eat healthier food

The United Nations

Leaders from more than 120 countries gather at the U.N. General Assembly.

Imagine if a person from every single country in the world got together in one room to talk about the world's problems. That is pretty much what happens at the United Nations.

The U.N. was started in 1945, at the end of World War II. Millions of people had died in the war, and world leaders wanted to stop anything like that from ever happening again. Representatives from 51 nations met in San Francisco and formed a worldwide organization to promote peace.

Today there are 193 countries in the U.N. Every year, each country sends a representative to New York City. The representatives come up with ideas for settling conflicts, fighting disease, and helping countries after natural disasters.

Flying the Flag
The U.N. flag shows the world surrounded by two olive branches, which are symbols of peace.

MANY TONGUES

There are thousands of languages spoken around the world. A speech at the U.N. is given in one of six official languages: English, French, Spanish, Russian, Arabic, or Chinese.

Interpreters translate the speech into each of the other five languages. Representatives listen to the translated speech through earphones. The job of translating that fast is so tiring that the interpreters only work 20 minutes at a time.

THE SECURITY COUNCIL

The most powerful group at the U.N. is the Security Council. The five permanent members of the council are the United States, France, Russia, the United Kingdom, and China. The council can vote to take military action or to punish countries that are behaving badly.

The World Is Getting Smaller

The world is not actually getting smaller but it sometimes feels that way.

Centuries ago, people had a harder time exchanging culture. It could take weeks to travel from the United States to another continent. Once there, Americans might not be able to communicate with the locals. Each country had its own music, food, and language.

All of this started changing as airplanes went up into the sky and computers went online. Now people and information can zoom around the world. This close connection between cultures is known as globalization.

Here are just a few examples of how America has imported and exported culture as the world has globalized.

IMPORTS

EMOJI
Emoji are images that people use in text messages, like this 😊 and this 🖤 and this 👍. They were invented in 1999 in Japan and are named after the Japanese words for picture (e-) and character (moji). Americans use emoji hundreds of times per second.

CHOW MEIN
Immigrants to America have brought recipes from their home countries. America now has more Chinese food restaurants than Burger Kings.

DIWALI
Diwali (pronounced dih-WAH-lee) is a holiday that comes from India. People who practice the Hindu religion celebrate this festival of lights in mid-November. Today there are more than 2 million Hindus in the U.S., and there are Diwali celebrations all over the country.

EXPORTS

ENGLISH
English is the primary language in only a handful of countries, yet nearly a quarter of the people in the world can speak and understand basic English. That's more than a billion people.

McDONALD'S
McDonald's is a good example of an American restaurant that has gone global. In 1948, there was just one McDonald's, in San Bernardino, California. There are now McDonald's restaurants operating in more than 100 countries.

AMERICAN FILMS
Many of the movies made in Hollywood, California, sell more tickets abroad than they do in the U.S. Today, if you meet someone from Russia, there's a good chance you've seen some of the same movies.

A World of Entertainment

The Avengers: Age of Ultron

Actress Marilyn Monroe

Pop star Beyoncé

Actors Leonardo DiCaprio and Kate Winslet in the blockbuster *Titanic*

Director Steven Spielberg

America is the world's entertainer. The United States produces more media and entertainment than any other country in the world. Movies, TV programs, commercials, hit songs, radio shows, and games made in America make people laugh and cry all over the planet.

All of these types of media are part of what is known as popular culture—or pop culture for short.

A diplomat is someone who represents his or her country abroad. Usually when people talk about American diplomats, they're speaking about serious political figures like Thomas Jefferson, who

Pop icon Madonna

Star Wars: The Force Awakens

AVATAR

The top-grossing movie of all time is *Avatar*, a 2009 Hollywood fantasy flick about a future world where humans mingle with big blue creatures. Almost 75% of all the tickets were sold overseas.

ELVIS PRESLEY

The King of Rock 'N' Roll strummed his way into hearts all over the world. The boy from Tupelo, Mississippi, sang hits like "Hound Dog" and "All Shook Up," topping music charts in countries from Australia to Italy.

OSCARS

Film stars around the world yearn to win one of the gold statues that are handed out in Hollywood each year to celebrate the year's best movies. The Oscars also celebrate films from other countries. Since 1956, the Academy of Motion Pictures and Sciences has given out an award for the best foreign language film.

BAYWATCH

Baywatch, a drama about lifeguards, has been broadcast in more than 100 countries. When the show was at its most popular in the 1990s, it had an audience of a billion people.

LEBRON JAMES

NBA basketball player LeBron James is famous pretty much everywhere. The finals of the NBA championship have been broadcast in 47 different languages in more than 150 countries.

represented the U.S. in France. But each song or movie that travels from the U.S. to other countries is a diplomat, too. These pieces of pop culture teach other countries about American life.

Chapter 12

AMERICA'S HOMEGROWN GIFTS TO THE WORLD

Think of all the fruits and vegetables lined end to end in the produce aisle of every grocery store. Do you see juicy green limes? There are almost no limes grown in the United States and yet almost every grocery store has limes for sale. How is that possible? Trade! Mexico sends limes that their farmers grow to America, and America sends corn that our farmers grow to Mexico. Trading gives everyone more choices, not just about which foods to eat, but also which clothes to wear, or which kind of car to drive.

Trading is not the only way countries can share their cultures. Music and sports that originated in one country can become popular all around the world. Basketball, for example, was invented in the United States, but today countries on every continent have gotten into the game.

The world often looks to the United States for innovations in music, TV, sports, film, and food. Turn the page to discover more of America's gifts to the world.

The Columbian Exchange

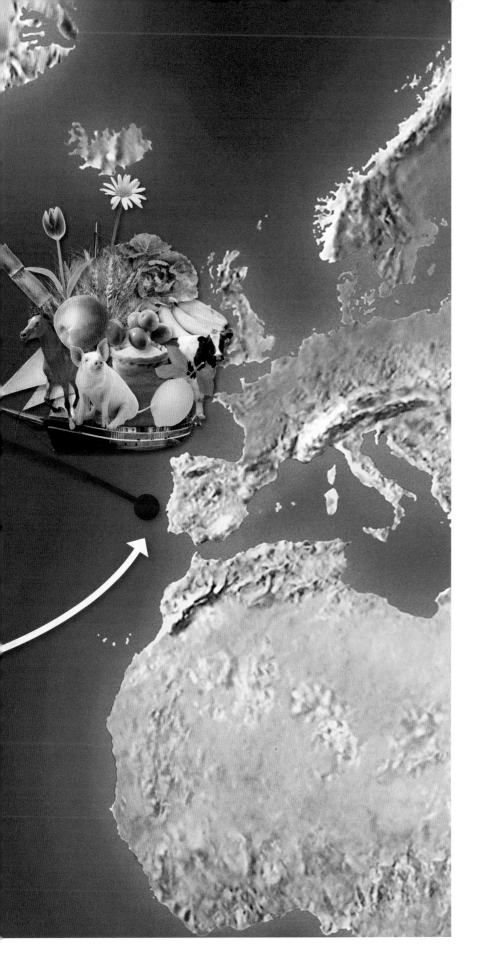

The explorer Christopher Columbus wasn't the first person to set foot in America, but his journey did start an important new era. After his trip in 1492, Europe and its colonies in America started trading all kinds of items, from bell peppers to bananas. Soon both places were enjoying plants and animals they'd never seen before.

FROM THE AMERICAS TO EUROPE

Avocados
Bell Peppers
Chili Peppers
Cotton
Chocolate (Cacao)
Corn
Marigolds
Peanuts
Pineapples
Potatoes
Pumpkins
Sunflowers
Tobacco
Turkeys

FROM EUROPE TO THE AMERICAS

Bananas
Chickens
Cows
Daisies
Horses
Lemons
Lettuce
Olives
Peaches
Pigs
Rice
Sugarcane
Tulips
Wheat

American Made

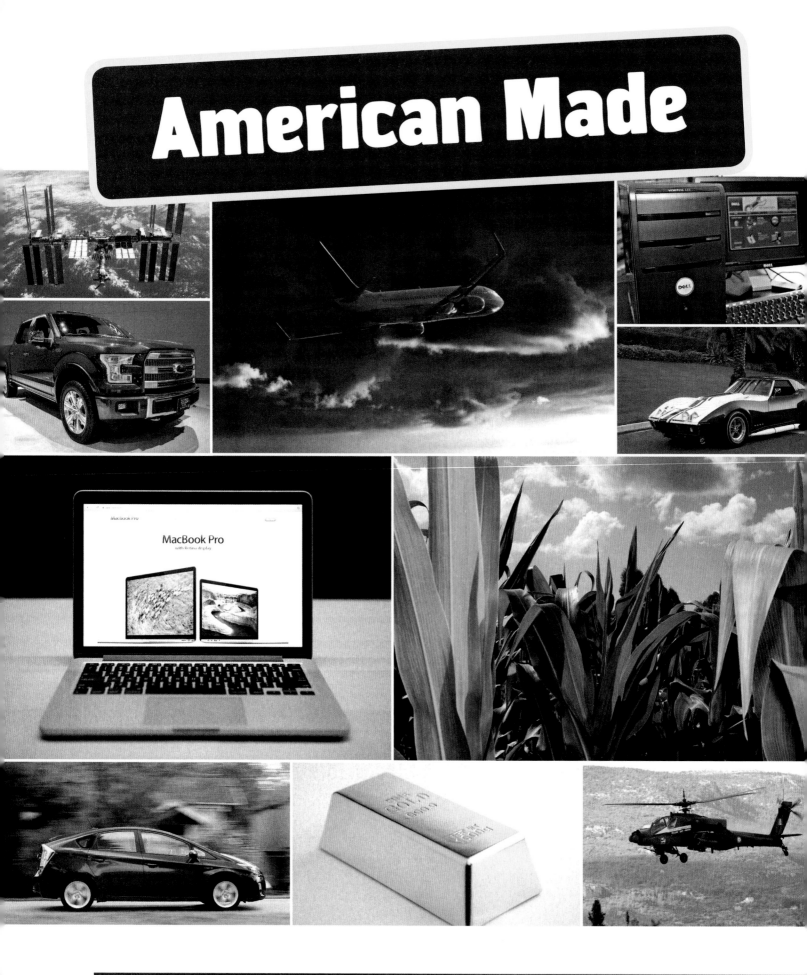

When America ships goods to other countries, those goods are called exports. Here are some of the most popular American exports.

Cars

The United States ships more than two million cars to other countries each year. The U.S. also imports tons of cars from countries worldwide.

Aircraft

More than 150,000 people work at Boeing, a company based in Chicago that makes planes, helicopters, and other aircraft. This American company doesn't just send its crafts to other countries. Boeing also sends its machines into space! The company helped to build the International Space Station.

Gold

The 1849 Gold Rush is long over but there are still plenty of gold mines in the United States. The mines producing the most gold are in western states, such as Alaska and Nevada. This precious metal is used to make electronics, jewelry and medicine. It can even be made into false teeth.

Computers

Japanese companies like Sony and Panasonic come to mind when many people think of electronics. But America churns out top-notch devices too. Computer companies, including Dell and Gateway, make many of their laptops in the U.S. and sell them in other countries.

Corn

More corn is grown in America than in any other country in the world. The state of Iowa alone grows three times the amount of corn that the whole country of Mexico grows. Every year, farmers harvest the plants in the fall. The corn is eaten by people from Peru to Taiwan.

CROPPING UP

Here are some popular crops that American farmers produce each year.

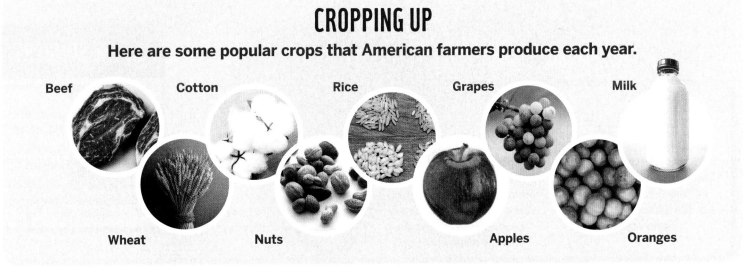

Beef · Cotton · Rice · Grapes · Milk · Wheat · Nuts · Apples · Oranges

American Music

B.B. King was a legendary blues guitarist and singer.

Singin' the Blues

Blues songs might sound sad, but this music has actually helped people cope in hard times. Blues music is often slow and soulful. Musicians pluck guitars and sing silky notes. The style evolved from songs that early African-Americans would sing when working in the fields—often as slaves.

The Blues came out of the American South around 1900. It emerged from places like Texas, Mississippi, and Louisiana. African-American people sang songs as a way of putting their years of suffering into words and to keep their spirits up. Blues inspired other types of music that would come later, like rock 'n' roll and jazz.

The blues musician B.B. King sang a song called "Every Day I Have the Blues." While his fingers raced along the guitar to happy notes, he sang sad words. This tension is what makes the blues a powerful form of expression. And it made B.B. King the king of the blues.

BLUES INSTRUMENTS
1. Guitar
2. Harmonica
3. Piano
4. Upright Bass
5. Drums

JAZZ INSTRUMENTS
1. Trumpet
2. Saxophone
3. Guitar
4. Piano
5. Upright bass
6. Drums

All That Jazz!

African-Americans created jazz in the early 1900s, in towns like New Orleans. Jazz musicians took soothing blues and mixed it with upbeat ragtime and marching band music. The result is a style that's all about rhythm and improvisation. When musicians decide what to play without planning it beforehand, that's known as improvising.

Early jazz musicians would take a well-known piece of music like "When the Saints Go Marching In" and throw in extra notes. They'd play a low note when they were supposed to play a high one. They'd take a long note and play it as five short ones. Listeners could still recognize the melody, but the song felt new.

America Goes Country

Early country music was played by mountain-dwellers in the hills of Appalachia and westerners in Texas towns. The musicians took the folk songs of English and Scottish immigrants and gave them a twang!

The Grand Ole Opry opened in Nashville, Tennessee, in 1925. Musicians from little towns, including Garth Brooks (above), came to play on the big stage. The city became known as America's country music capital. Soon people around the U.S. were tapping their toes to "honky tonk" beats.

COUNTRY INSTRUMENTS
1. Accordion
2. Banjo
3. Guitar
4. Fiddle
5. Washboard
6. Bass
7. Mandolin

ROCK INSTRUMENTS
1. Guitar
2. Bass
3. Drums

Hip to the Hop

A younger American music style inspired by the rhythms of jazz and blues is hip-hop. Hip-hop is the older cousin of rap music. Rather than sing, hip-hop musicians speak or rap over beats and melodies. Some of the earliest hip-hop rappers came out of the Bronx in the 1970s. They rhymed in time in grand slam jams. The Sugar Hill Gang (below) gets the credit for bringing rap to the masses with their 1979 hit "Rapper's Delight." The 14-minute single in which the trio brags about money and mic skills sold millions of copies. The hip-to-the-hop song paved the way for future rap artists and still moves feet today.

All Shook Up

Rock 'n' roll exploded onto the scene in the 1950s. Singers like Elvis Presley (above), dubbed the King of Rock 'n' Roll, popularized this new sound, a mix of rhythm and blues and country music. Parents thought the music was noise and a negative influence on teens, but it was clear that rock 'n' roll was here to stay.

America Eats

Take a trip around the United States for a sampling of its regions' most famous foods and drinks.

1. ALABAMA/MISSISSIPPI
Location: No particular city
Food: Biscuits and gravy
Fact: Restaurants in the Deep South serve up buttermilk biscuits covered in thick gravy for breakfast.

2. CALIFORNIA
Location: Hollywood, California
Food: Cobb salad
Fact: The Cobb salad was invented by restaurant owner Robert Cobb, who made the salad using leftovers. A classic Cobb includes tomato, bacon, eggs, and avocado.

3. GEORGIA
Location: Atlanta, Georgia
Food: Coca-Cola
Fact: In 1886, pharmacist John S. Pemberton invented the soft drink that would launch one of the world's best-known companies.

4. HAWAII
Location: No particular city
Food: Kalua pig
Fact: This Polynesian dish is eaten at Hawaiian feasts known as luaus (*loo*-ows).

5. ILLINOIS
Location: Chicago, Illinois
Food: Deep dish pizza
Fact: Chicago pizzerias have been serving up thick slices of deep-dish pizza since 1943.

6. KANSAS/MISSOURI
Location: Kansas City
Food: Barbecue
Fact: Kansas City-style BBQ is covered in sweet and tangy sauces. The meat might be pulled pork, beef brisket, or smoked turkey. This style of BBQ has been around since the early 1900s.

7. KENTUCKY
Location: Louisville
Food: Fried Chicken
Fact: Colonel Harland Sanders started cooking meals for hungry travelers in the 1930s, and by the 1960s he had 600 restaurants. Today, Kentucky Fried Chicken (KFC) sells American-style fried chicken in 115 countries.

8. LOUISIANA
Location: No particular city
Food: Jambalaya
Fact: Jambalaya is a dish that comes from Creole and Cajun cultures in Louisiana. These are American cultures with French and Spanish influences. The Creole version is "red jambalaya," a dish with meat, celery, onion, bell pepper, seafood, tomato, and rice.

9. MAINE/MASSACHUSETTS
Location: New England
Food: Clam chowder
Fact: New England clam chowder is a bowlful of shellfish, salt pork, onions, potatoes and milk. In the 1800s, writer Joseph C. Lincoln said it "is a dish to preach about, to chant praises and sing hymns and burn incense before."

10. NEBRASKA
Location: Omaha, Nebraska
Food: Reuben sandwich
Fact: Many believe Bernard Schimmel at 18 invented the Reuben sandwich— corned beef, sauerkraut, Thousand Island dressing, and Swiss cheese on rye bread—while working late at his father's hotel in Omaha.

11. NEW JERSEY
Location: Camden, New Jersey
Food: Campbell's soup
Fact: In 1869, the company that would become famous for its chicken noodle soup opened in Camden, New Jersey.

12. NEW YORK
Location: Buffalo, New York
Food: Buffalo wings
Fact: Before 1964, wings were considered the worst part of the chicken. Bar owner Teressa Bellissimo changed that when she invented buffalo wings in Buffalo, New York. She fried the wings, covered them in hot sauce and served them with celery and blue cheese dressing.

13. NORTH CAROLINA
Location: No particular city
Food: Barbeque
Fact: Barbeque is such a big

part of North Carolina culture that lawmakers have fought in the capital over which style is best! For decades restaurants in the Piedmont region have served BBQ with vinegar, pepper and tomato sauce.

14. OHIO
Location: Cincinnati, Ohio
Food: Chili
Fact: Cincinnati Chili has flavors of cinnamon and cloves. It's often served on spaghetti or on a hot dog, under a big pile of cheese.

15. PENNSYLVANIA
Location: Philadelphia, Pennsylvania
Food: Philly cheesesteak
Fact: This long crusty roll filled with beef and cheese has been a famous Philly treat since 1930.

16. TENNESSEE
Location: Nashville, Tennessee
Food: Cotton candy
Fact: In 1897, the dentist William James Morrison and his friend John C. Warton invented a machine that made cotton candy. They called their new treat "Fairy Floss."

17. TEXAS
Location: No particular city
Food: Tex-Mex
Fact: Tex-Mex is an American cuisine with Mexican, Spanish, and Native-American influences. Typical dishes include corn, beans, tortillas, and meat.

18. VERMONT
Location: Burlington, Vermont
Food: Ben & Jerry's ice cream
Fact: Ben Cohen & Jerry Greenfield opened their first ice cream shop out of an old gas station in Burlington, Vermont, in 1978. Now their ice cream is sold in 33 countries.

19. WASHINGTON
Location: Seattle, Washington
Food: Starbucks coffee
Fact: The first Starbucks coffee shop opened in Seattle in 1971. Starbuck is the first mate in Herman Melville's classic novel, *Moby Dick*.

20. WISCONSIN/MINNESOTA
Location: No particular city
Food: Cheese curds
Fact: Eateries in Wisconsin and Minnesota serve up chunks of soured milk, deep-fried and topped with garlic or other herbs.

Chapter 13

ONE OF A KIND

Like the sayings on these pages, the people, places, animals, and everyday things you'll learn about in this chapter are quintessentially American. You might even say they're as American as apple pie.

All thumbs

Let's get this show on the road!

When pigs fly

In a nutshell

Talk Like an American

H as anyone ever told you to break a leg? It might sound like a rude comment, but it is actually a way of wishing someone good luck before a performance. An expression that means something different from what the words seem to say is called an idiom.

You may have also heard these expressions: All thumbs. Back to square one. Let's get this show on the road!

Sayings like these get handed down over generations, even if the stories behind them got lost along the way.

Here are some phrases the State Department put together for foreigners who are trying to learn American English. Some of them were handed down to America from English people who settled here. Try to use them in everyday speech. It's a piece of cake!

all thumbs: uncoordinated and awkward, especially with one's hands

as the crow flies: directly or in a straight line

go back to square one: return to the beginning of any activity

bad blood: negative or ill feelings

bend over backwards: to do whatever one can to help

the big cheese: an important, powerful person

bite the bullet: face a difficult or unpleasant situation

change horses in midstream: change plans or leaders in the middle of some event

dead to the world: fast asleep

eager beaver: a person who is excited and enthusiastic about something

fair-weather friend: a person who is loyal in good times but is not when times get hard

get this show on the road: get started

have the last laugh: outsmart or get revenge on someone who thinks he or she has been clever

in a nutshell: in a few words

keep one's fingers crossed: hope for something

kick the bucket: die

let the cat out of the bag: reveal a secret

monkey business: mischievous activity

out of the blue: suddenly and unexpectedly

pop the question: ask someone to get married

walking on air: blissfully happy

when pigs fly: a way of saying that something will never happen

American Journeys

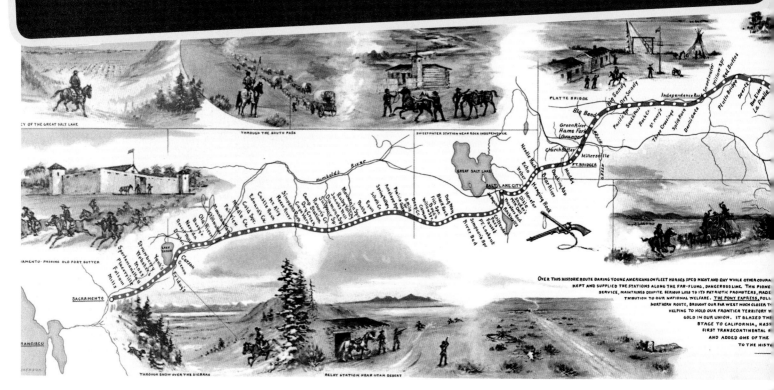

The Pony Express

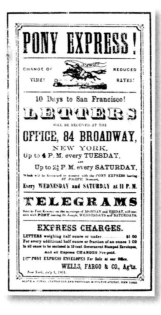

The Pony Express was the most thrilling postal route in American history. On April 3, 1860, brave riders took off on horses from St. Joseph, Missouri and Sacramento, California. Their task was to trade mail between the East and West. Before the Pony Express, it could take months to trade letters.

Riders would go as fast as they could from one station to the next. They'd trade their exhausted horses for fresh ones and keep riding. They had to risk their lives. There was harsh weather and little water. Sometimes American Indians or bandits would attack them. The service operated for only 18 months, but the riders became famous for their courage.

This map shows the route followed by the Pony Express. (Below left) An 1895 advertisement boasts the speediness of the Pony Express.

9 DAYS, 23 HOURS
The time it took the first Pony Express to travel east to west

11 DAYS, 12 HOURS
The time it took the first Pony Express to travel west to east

GET YOUR KICKS ON ROUTE 66

America's first paved highway was a two-lane road stretching from Chicago, Illinois, to Santa Monica, California. In the 1920s, the "Mother Road" of America got its name: Route 66. Today, the road reminds people of a romantic American idea.

Route 66 attracted writers, adventurers, and people looking for a better life out West, the same way pioneers and gold-seekers had hoped the West would seal their fortunes. Eventually so many people were driving on the road that the two-lane highway had to be replaced with something bigger. Route 66 is no longer completely intact, but people can still visit historic sites that the original travelers saw on their way to sunny California.

2,448
Miles the road spanned from Chicago, Illinois, to Springfield, Missouri, to Santa Monica, California

85%
Portion of Route 66 that is still drivable today

Hot Spots

MOUNT RUSHMORE, KEYSTONE, SOUTH DAKOTA
It took 400 men 14 years to carve the heads of Presidents George Washington, Thomas Jefferson, Theodore Roosevelt, and Abraham Lincoln into the Black Hills.

THE STRIP: LAS VEGAS, NEVADA
The lights are bright on this five-mile strip of Las Vegas. Gamblers roll the dice at casinos. Families go to glitzy shows featuring magicians and acrobats.

THE GATEWAY ARCH: ST. LOUIS, MISSOURI
The Arch in St. Louis was built in honor of Thomas Jefferson, who doubled the size of the U.S. while he was president. The 630-foot structure is known as the "Gateway to the West" because it celebrates the westward expansion of America.

GOLDEN GATE BRIDGE: SAN FRANCISCO, CALIFORNIA
The giant rust-colored bridge in San Francisco has been open to cars since 1937. It connects the peninsula city with land to the north.

WAIKIKI BEACH: HAWAII
Waikiki is a Hawaiian word meaning "spouting water." It was named for the rivers and springs that flow nearby. Today more than 4 million people from around the world visit to swim, snorkel, and surf.

MACKINAC BRIDGE: MACKINAW CITY, MICHIGAN

This bridge is one of the world's longest bridges. High winds can move the middle of it 35 feet in either direction.

About 75 million people from around the world visit the United States each year. An even greater number of Americans travel around the U.S. to discover new parts of their country. Here are some of the top tourist spots.

MILLENNIUM PARK: CHICAGO, ILLINOIS

The land the park stands on was once covered with railroad tracks and parking lots. Now this park in the center of town is filled with art and gardens.

THE WHITE HOUSE: WASHINGTON, D.C.

Each day, about 6,000 people visit the home where the U.S. president lives and works. The home has 132 rooms and 35 bathrooms!

TIMES SQUARE: NEW YORK CITY, NEW YORK

Every year, more than 39 million people flock to Times Square. They come to see the neon lights and to soak up the energy of the city that never sleeps.

WALT DISNEY WORLD: ORLANDO, FLORIDA

This theme park is the size of San Francisco and known for its wild rides. Another draw? Tourists can get their pictures taken with Mickey Mouse, Goofy, and other Disney characters.

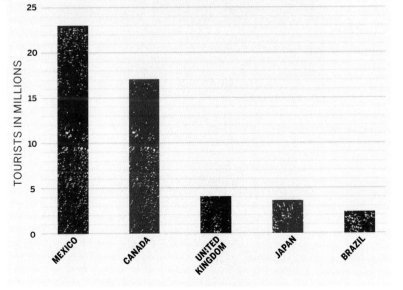

TOP TOURISTS

Here are the top five foreign countries that tourists come to America from.

TOURISTS IN MILLIONS

MEXICO — CANADA — UNITED KINGDOM — JAPAN — BRAZIL

The skeleton of a T. rex named Sue stands in the Field Museum in Chicago, Illinois.

$8.4 million
The amount the Field Museum paid to buy Sue

42 feet
The length Sue stretches from head to tail

12 feet
How tall Sue is at her hips

250
The number of bones and teeth in Sue's skeleton

67 million
Years since dinosaurs were alive in what is now North America

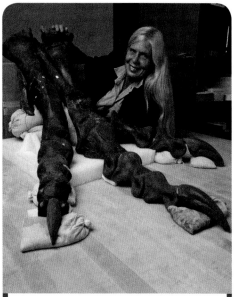

Sue is named for Sue Hendrickson, the woman who discovered the dinosaur bones on a digging trip in South Dakota in 1990.

A Dinosaur Named Sue

The most complete Tyrannosaurus rex skeleton in the world is owned by the Field Museum in Chicago. Her name is Sue.

Before Sue, scientists had never assembled more than 60% of a T. rex. Sue has 90% of her bones! Because she's so complete, Sue can better teach scientists about what the world was like when giant flesh-eaters roamed North America.

America's Bird

Bald eagles fly only in the skies of North America. The birds aren't actually bald. Their heads are covered in snowy white feathers. For thousands of years, eagles have been symbols of strength. This particular species of eagle became America's unofficial national bird in 1782, when Congress approved a national seal featuring the animal.

6 FEET TO 8 FEET
The wingspan of a bald eagle

20 FEET
The height of the biggest bald eagle's nest ever found

2007
The year the bald eagle was taken off the endangered species list

SEAL OF THE UNITED STATES

It took six years for the Founding Fathers to decide on America's seal. Check out the early designs and eventual winner.

1776   1780   1782

Front   Back

PRESIDENTIAL PARDON

The eagle may be America's national bird, but only one feathered creature gets its own ceremony at the White House. Every November, the president "pardons" a turkey. The freed bird is sent to a farm where it can gobble out the rest of its days in peace.

Old Faithful

A CAUTIONARY TALE

Even when it's not exploding, the water in a geyser is hotter than boiling. If visitors aren't careful, geysers can be deadly. Twenty people have lost their lives to the scalding waters in Yellowstone.

Every hour or two, Old Faithful erupts in the middle of Yellowstone National Park in Wyoming. Boiling hot water shoots out of the geyser and 180 feet in the air! Geysers are vents in the earth's surface that blow out steam in order to balance the earth's temperature.

More than half of the world's geysers are in Yellowstone National Park. Watching them erupt is thrilling and frightening. Old Faithful isn't the biggest geyser, but it is the biggest geyser that erupts on a regular schedule. Park rangers have been studying Old Faithful for so long that they can predict the exact time it will blow 90% of the time.

YOU KNOW YELLOWSTONE

Yellowstone is America's first and oldest park. It was established in 1872.

Yellowstone is the only place in the world where wild bison have survived since primitive times.

Yellowstone spans three states: 96% is in Wyoming, 3% is in Montana, and 1% is in Idaho.

Other Natural Wonders

A SEA OF SAND

In New Mexico, hills of white sand stretch for miles in every direction. White Sands National Monument is the world's largest field of gypsum sand. The grains constantly move in the wind, forming dunes of 10 to 60 feet high that ripple over the horizon like waves. Visitors can walk up the dunes and even "sand board" down, just as snowboarders slide down icy slopes.

A GIANT RIVER

Many people believe the Everglades is a swamp. But this giant wetland in Florida is actually a slow moving river. The grasslands here are so vast that some call the Everglades the "river of grass." Some of the grass blades are so sharp that they can cut through your clothing!

The varieties of plants and animals living in the Everglades don't coexist anywhere else on the planet. This is the only place where alligators and crocodiles swim side by side.

← CROCODILE OR ALLIGATOR? →

If you saw one in the wild, you'd probably run away before you could examine them. But here are some tips for distinguishing an American alligator from an American crocodile.

	COLOR	TEETH	SNOUT
ALLIGATOR	Black	Big tooth sticks out	Broad, round
CROCODILE	Gray-green	Teeth mostly hidden	Narrow, long

Money Matters

Each government issues its own money. Money usually consists of paper notes and coins that people can exchange for goods and services. America's money is made by skilled people who work with special equipment at the U.S. Treasury. The bills are made of cotton and linen instead of the wood pulp of which most paper is made. That's why nothing else feels quite like money.

The U.S. Treasury prints bills in sheets covered in green and black ink. Then machines cut the bills apart. Each bill and coin has its own special symbols.

PENNY

- The one-cent coin is made of copper and zinc.
- The profile of Abraham Lincoln, the 16th president, is stamped on the penny.
- Lincoln's face has been on the penny since 1909. Before then there were other figures, such as a lady with flowing hair who symbolized liberty.
- The Lincoln memorial appears on the back of most pennies.

NICKEL

- The five-cent coin is made of the metal nickel. That's where the coin got its name.
- The face of Thomas Jefferson, the third president, is stamped on the nickel.
- The building on the back is Monticello, Jefferson's historic home in Virginia.
- The motto "In God We Trust" started appearing on coins during the Civil War.

DIME

- The ten-cent coin is the smallest and thinnest coin.
- The face of Franklin D. Roosevelt, the 32nd president, is stamped on the dime.
- Roosevelt's image appeared on the dime soon after he died in 1945.
- On the back is a torch, which stands for liberty. There is also an olive branch for peace and an oak branch for strength.

QUARTER

- George Washington's face has appeared on the twenty-five cent coin since 1932. For many years, there was no face on the quarter at all.
- Quarters were once made of silver. Now they're made of copper and covered in nickel.
- The back shows an eagle and the U.S. motto, "E Pluribus Unum." That's Latin for "out of many, one."

LESS COMMON COINS

Sacajawea Golden Dollar
A one-dollar coin shows Sacajawea, a Shoshone Indian woman who helped explorers Meriwether Lewis and William Clark. Lewis and Clark were the first explorers to make it to the West Coast.

John F. Kennedy Half Dollar
A coin worth fifty cents shows the image of President John F. Kennedy, the 35th president.

ON THE MONEY

Each U.S. bill shows a president or other important American figure. Bills worth more than $100 are rarely used. The government no longer prints them.

$1
President George Washington

$2
President Thomas Jefferson

$5
President Abraham Lincoln

$10
Alexander Hamilton

$20
President Andrew Jackson

$50
President Ulysses S. Grant

$100
Benjamin Franklin

$500
President William McKinley

$1,000
President Grover Cleveland

$5,000
President James Madison

$10,000
Samuel P. Chase, a former U.S. Secretary of the Treasury

$100,000
President Woodrow Wilson

The Freedom Tower

After terrorists destroyed the Twin Towers on 9/11, the part of Manhattan where the buildings had stood became known as Ground Zero. (This is usually the name for the site of a nuclear explosion.) Americans decided to to rebuild the World Trade Center even bigger than it was before.

Construction on the 104-story tower began in 2006. An army of 10,000 workers hauled and hammered for years. The building needed 48,000 tons of steel. People call the building the "Freedom Tower," even though that is not its official name. It has become a symbol of our country's resilience.

In 2014, One World Trade Center opened. The tip-top of the building reaches 1,776 feet. 1776 was the year America declared independence from Britain.

THE TWIN POOLS

Two memorial pools are in the spot where the World Trade Center towers used to be. Engraved on the sides are the names of those who died in the 9/11 attacks.

Inside One World Trade Center

One World Trade Center is the tallest building in all of North and South America. This diagram shows what went into the tower.

THE SPIRE
Rising more than 30 stories above the roof, the spire includes an antenna and a lightning rod.

We remember
We rebuild
We come back stronger!

President Barack Obama signed one of the final steel beams placed on the 104th floor.

THE BASE
There are no windows for 186 feet. The concrete around the base is 5.5 feet thick.

Thick concrete

UNDERGROUND
Below the ground, 27 columns support the foundation of the tower.

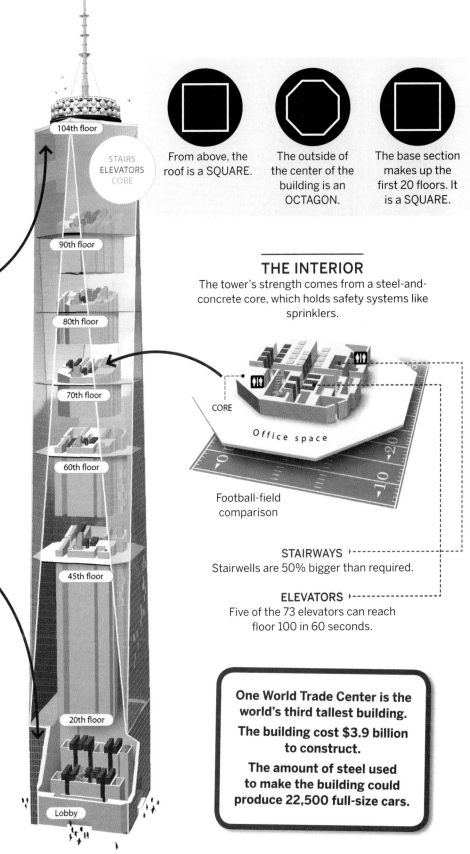

104th floor

STAIRS ELEVATORS CORE

90th floor

80th floor

70th floor

60th floor

45th floor

20th floor

Lobby

From above, the roof is a SQUARE.

The outside of the center of the building is an OCTAGON.

The base section makes up the first 20 floors. It is a SQUARE.

THE INTERIOR
The tower's strength comes from a steel-and-concrete core, which holds safety systems like sprinklers.

CORE

Office space

Football-field comparison

STAIRWAYS
Stairwells are 50% bigger than required.

ELEVATORS
Five of the 73 elevators can reach floor 100 in 60 seconds.

One World Trade Center is the world's third tallest building.

The building cost $3.9 billion to construct.

The amount of steel used to make the building could produce 22,500 full-size cars.

Chapter 14

YEAR BY YEAR

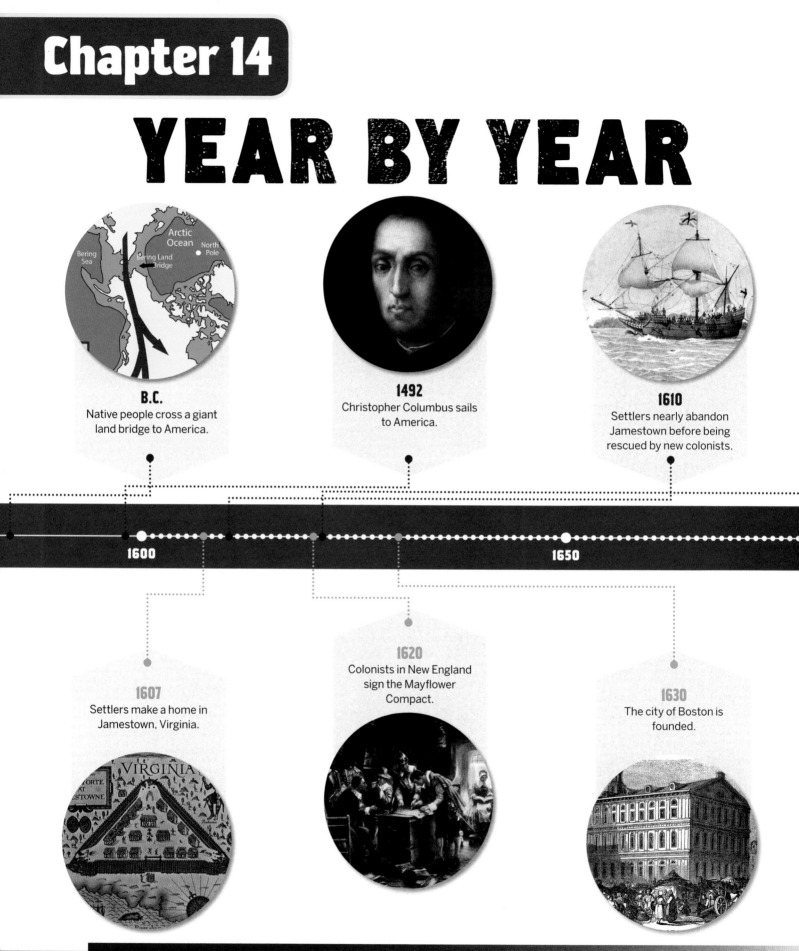

B.C.
Native people cross a giant land bridge to America.

1492
Christopher Columbus sails to America.

1610
Settlers nearly abandon Jamestown before being rescued by new colonists.

1600

1650

1607
Settlers make a home in Jamestown, Virginia.

1620
Colonists in New England sign the Mayflower Compact.

1630
The city of Boston is founded.

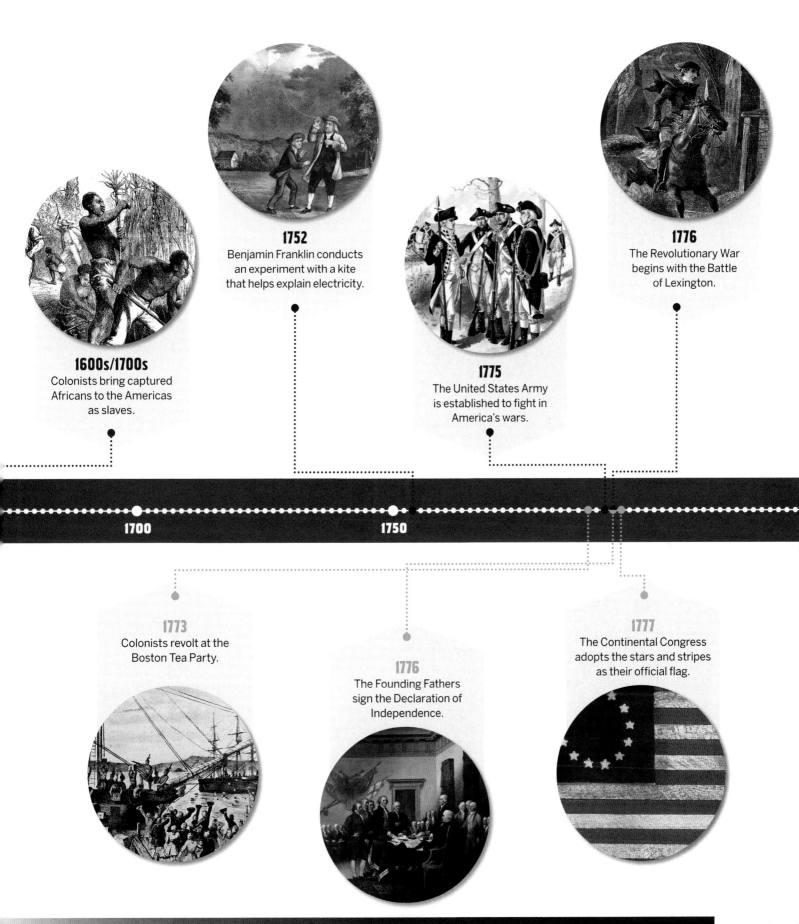

1600s/1700s
Colonists bring captured Africans to the Americas as slaves.

1752
Benjamin Franklin conducts an experiment with a kite that helps explain electricity.

1775
The United States Army is established to fight in America's wars.

1776
The Revolutionary War begins with the Battle of Lexington.

1700

1750

1773
Colonists revolt at the Boston Tea Party.

1776
The Founding Fathers sign the Declaration of Independence.

1777
The Continental Congress adopts the stars and stripes as their official flag.

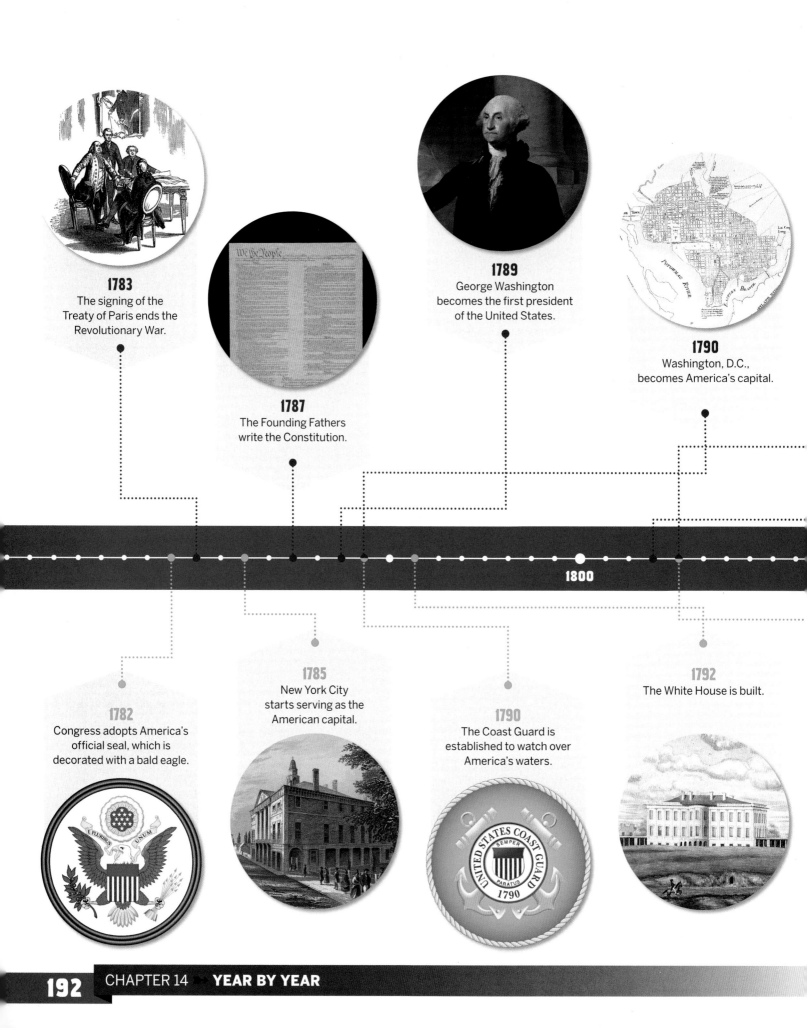

1783
The signing of the Treaty of Paris ends the Revolutionary War.

1787
The Founding Fathers write the Constitution.

1789
George Washington becomes the first president of the United States.

1790
Washington, D.C., becomes America's capital.

1800

1782
Congress adopts America's official seal, which is decorated with a bald eagle.

1785
New York City starts serving as the American capital.

1790
The Coast Guard is established to watch over America's waters.

1792
The White House is built.

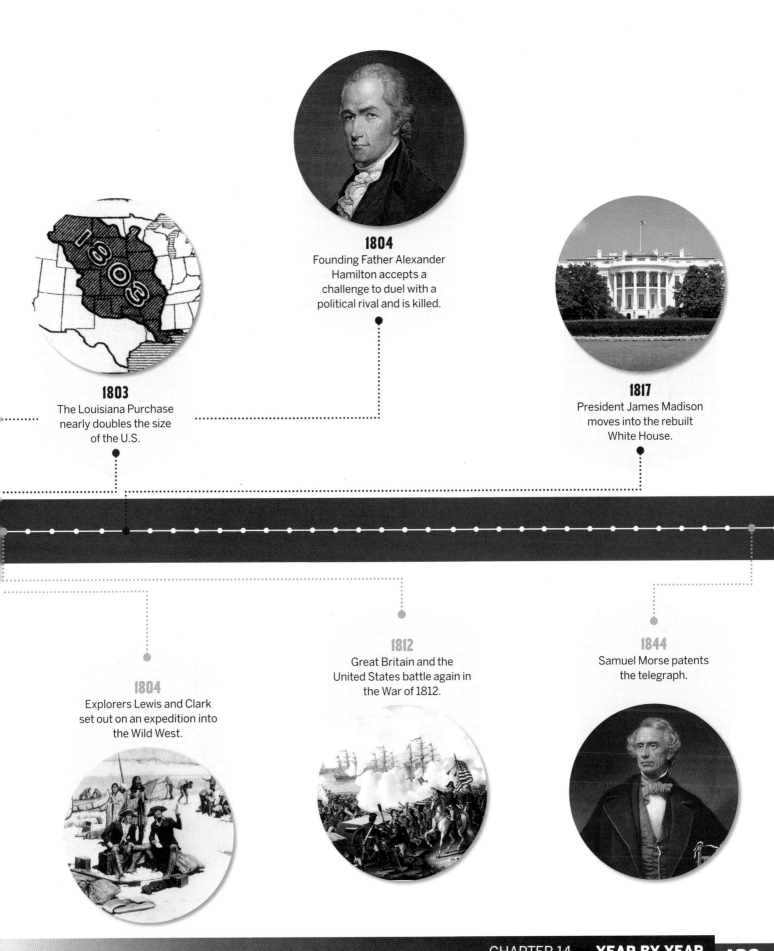

1804
Founding Father Alexander Hamilton accepts a challenge to duel with a political rival and is killed.

1803
The Louisiana Purchase nearly doubles the size of the U.S.

1817
President James Madison moves into the rebuilt White House.

1804
Explorers Lewis and Clark set out on an expedition into the Wild West.

1812
Great Britain and the United States battle again in the War of 1812.

1844
Samuel Morse patents the telegraph.

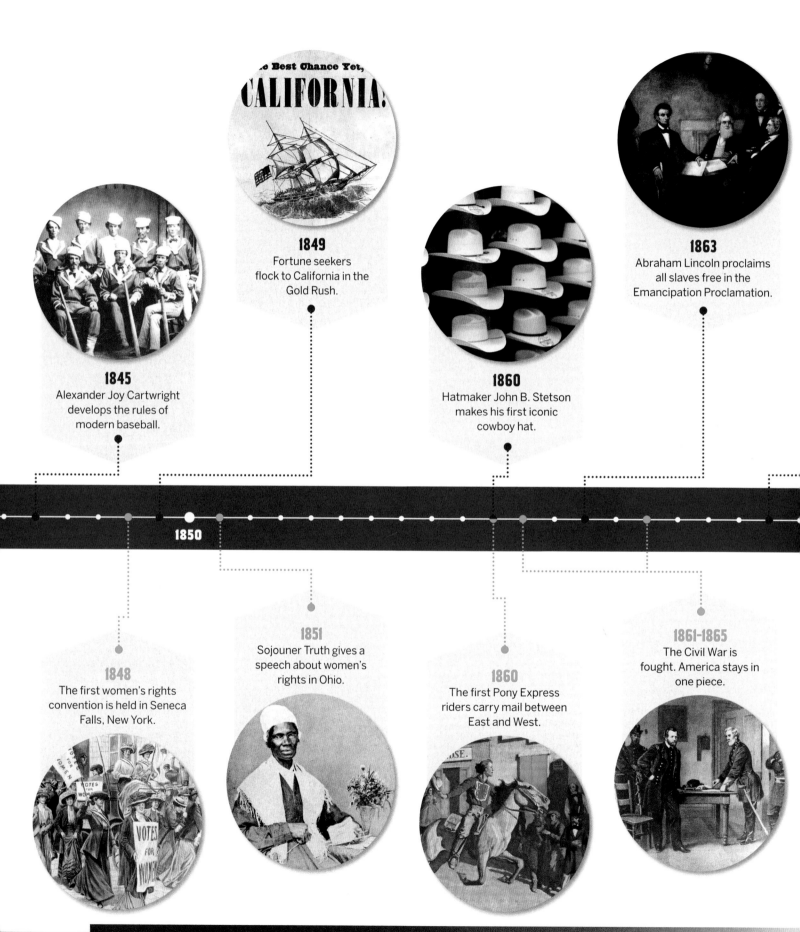

1845
Alexander Joy Cartwright develops the rules of modern baseball.

1849
Fortune seekers flock to California in the Gold Rush.

1860
Hatmaker John B. Stetson makes his first iconic cowboy hat.

1863
Abraham Lincoln proclaims all slaves free in the Emancipation Proclamation.

1850

1848
The first women's rights convention is held in Seneca Falls, New York.

1851
Sojouner Truth gives a speech about women's rights in Ohio.

1860
The first Pony Express riders carry mail between East and West.

1861-1865
The Civil War is fought. America stays in one piece.

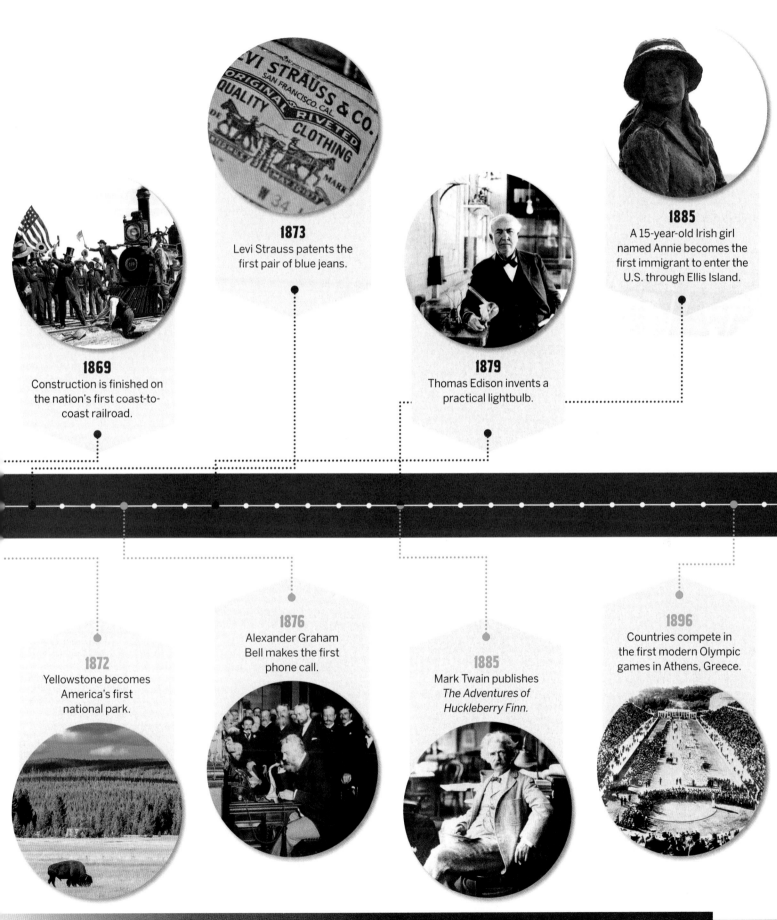

1869
Construction is finished on the nation's first coast-to-coast railroad.

1873
Levi Strauss patents the first pair of blue jeans.

1879
Thomas Edison invents a practical lightbulb.

1885
A 15-year-old Irish girl named Annie becomes the first immigrant to enter the U.S. through Ellis Island.

1872
Yellowstone becomes America's first national park.

1876
Alexander Graham Bell makes the first phone call.

1885
Mark Twain publishes *The Adventures of Huckleberry Finn.*

1896
Countries compete in the first modern Olympic games in Athens, Greece.

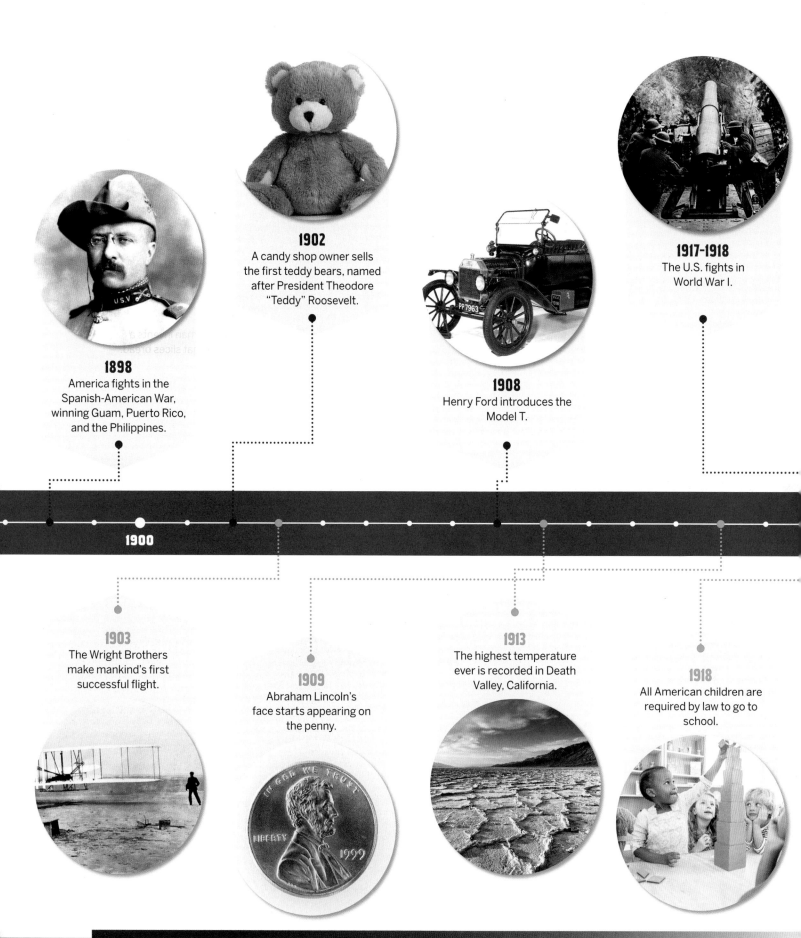

1898
America fights in the Spanish-American War, winning Guam, Puerto Rico, and the Philippines.

1902
A candy shop owner sells the first teddy bears, named after President Theodore "Teddy" Roosevelt.

1908
Henry Ford introduces the Model T.

1917-1918
The U.S. fights in World War I.

1900

1903
The Wright Brothers make mankind's first successful flight.

1909
Abraham Lincoln's face starts appearing on the penny.

1913
The highest temperature ever is recorded in Death Valley, California.

1918
All American children are required by law to go to school.

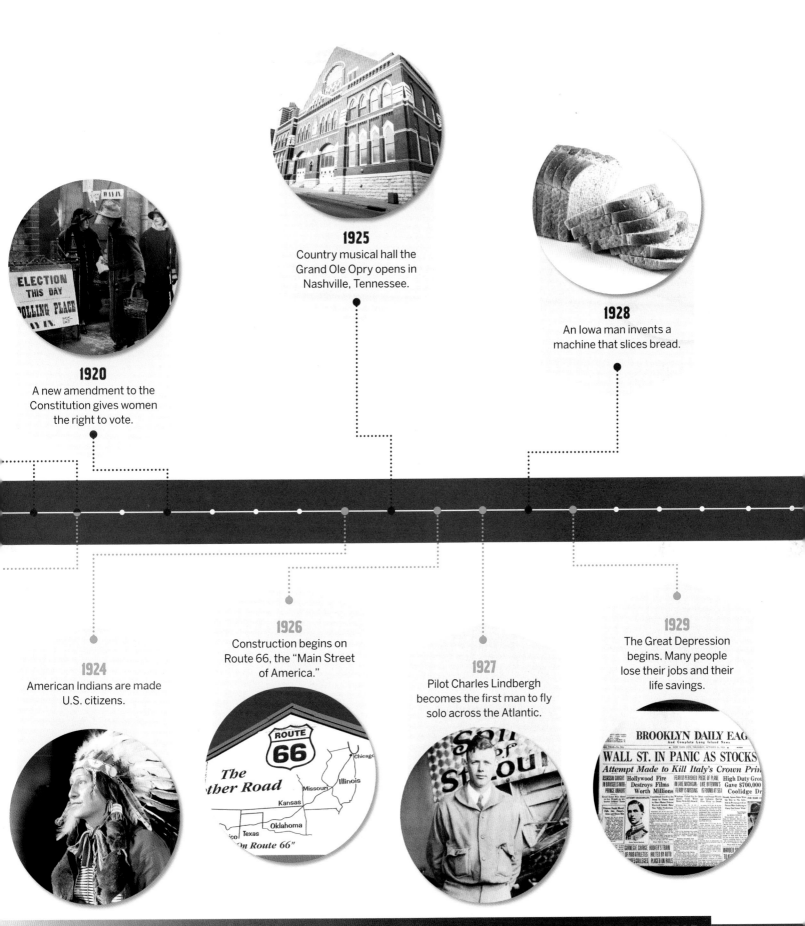

1925
Country musical hall the Grand Ole Opry opens in Nashville, Tennessee.

1928
An Iowa man invents a machine that slices bread.

1920
A new amendment to the Constitution gives women the right to vote.

1924
American Indians are made U.S. citizens.

1926
Construction begins on Route 66, the "Main Street of America."

1927
Pilot Charles Lindbergh becomes the first man to fly solo across the Atlantic.

1929
The Great Depression begins. Many people lose their jobs and their life savings.

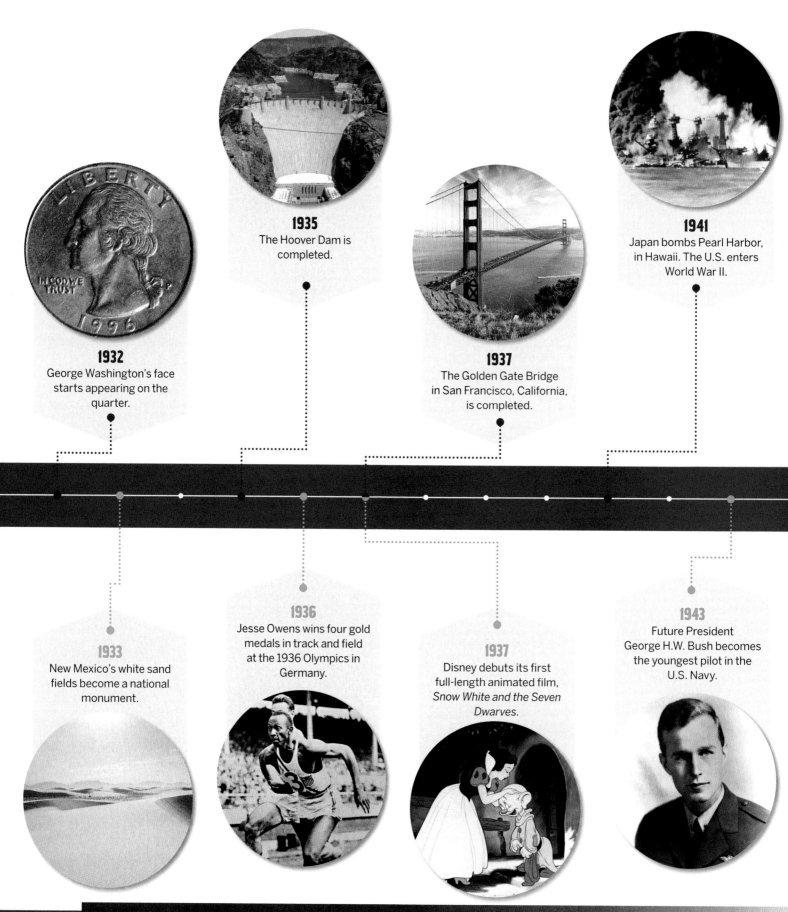

1935
The Hoover Dam is
completed.

1941
Japan bombs Pearl Harbor,
in Hawaii. The U.S. enters
World War II.

1932
George Washington's face
starts appearing on the
quarter.

1937
The Golden Gate Bridge
in San Francisco, California,
is completed.

1933
New Mexico's white sand
fields become a national
monument.

1936
Jesse Owens wins four gold
medals in track and field
at the 1936 Olympics in
Germany.

1937
Disney debuts its first
full-length animated film,
*Snow White and the Seven
Dwarves*.

1943
Future President
George H.W. Bush becomes
the youngest pilot in the
U.S. Navy.

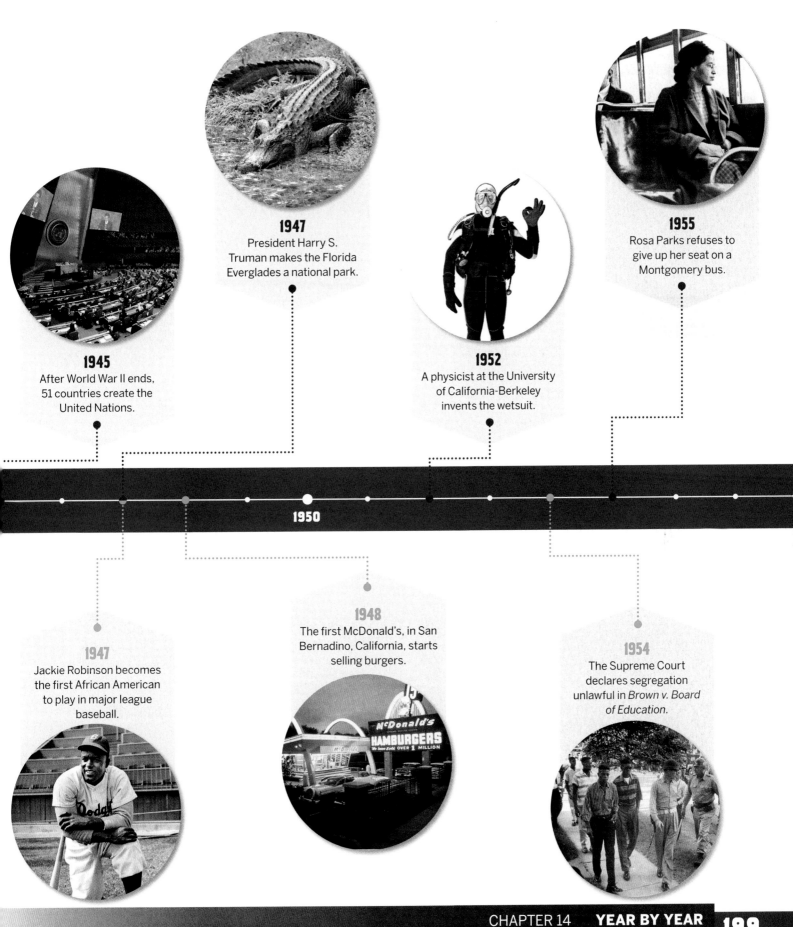

1945
After World War II ends, 51 countries create the United Nations.

1947
President Harry S. Truman makes the Florida Everglades a national park.

1952
A physicist at the University of California-Berkeley invents the wetsuit.

1955
Rosa Parks refuses to give up her seat on a Montgomery bus.

1950

1947
Jackie Robinson becomes the first African American to play in major league baseball.

1948
The first McDonald's, in San Bernadino, California, starts selling burgers.

1954
The Supreme Court declares segregation unlawful in *Brown v. Board of Education*.

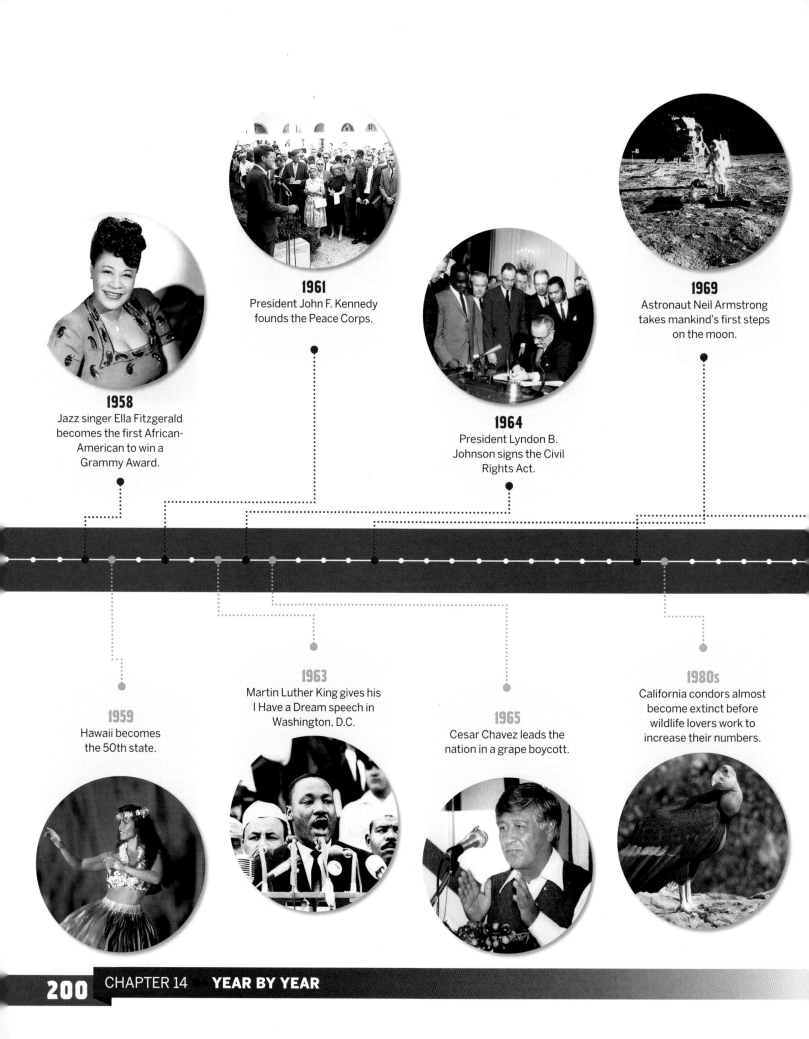

1961
President John F. Kennedy founds the Peace Corps.

1969
Astronaut Neil Armstrong takes mankind's first steps on the moon.

1958
Jazz singer Ella Fitzgerald becomes the first African-American to win a Grammy Award.

1964
President Lyndon B. Johnson signs the Civil Rights Act.

1959
Hawaii becomes the 50th state.

1963
Martin Luther King gives his I Have a Dream speech in Washington, D.C.

1965
Cesar Chavez leads the nation in a grape boycott.

1980s
California condors almost become extinct before wildlife lovers work to increase their numbers.

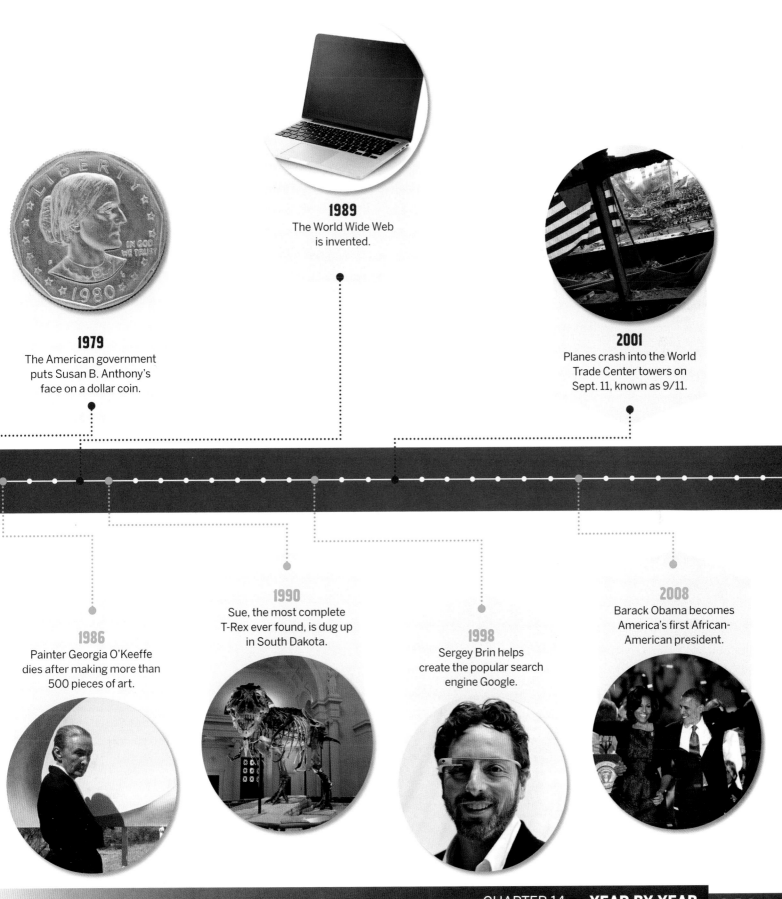

1979
The American government puts Susan B. Anthony's face on a dollar coin.

1989
The World Wide Web is invented.

2001
Planes crash into the World Trade Center towers on Sept. 11, known as 9/11.

1986
Painter Georgia O'Keeffe dies after making more than 500 pieces of art.

1990
Sue, the most complete T-Rex ever found, is dug up in South Dakota.

1998
Sergey Brin helps create the popular search engine Google.

2008
Barack Obama becomes America's first African-American president.

GLOSSARY

abolitionist: to abolish something means to get rid of it. Abolitionists were people who wanted to stop, or get rid of, slavery.

amendment: a change made to a document or law. To amend something means to alter it, often for the better.

assassinate: to kill someone, often in a planned attack and for political reasons.

boycott: to refuse to buy something or participate in something as a form of protest.

budget: the amount of money a person or group has to spend. When you have a surplus, that means you have more than you need.

citizen: a legal resident of a country who has the rights and protection of that country.

civil rights: the rights that every citizen should have, no matter who they are, where they come from, or what they look like.

colony/colonist: an area controlled by a country that is in a different place than that country. A *colonist* is someone who lives in a colony, sometimes after leaving the home country in search of a better or different life.

constitution: a document that explains the basic rules of a government and how it should work. When the word is capitalized—*Constitution*—it refers to the constitution of the United States. Individual states and other countries can also have their own constitutions.

culture: the customs or beliefs of a group or place.

democracy: a type of government in which the people help make choices about how it is run.

descendant: a person who is related to other people who lived in the past. To descend from someone means you are part of the same family tree, but they lived before you did.

discrimination: the practice of treating one person or group worse than another person or group, often because of their race or gender or some other quality. If someone is discriminated against, it means they are treated unfairly.

emancipate: to free someone from another person's control or influence.

ethnicity: a large group of people who share customs or characteristics. Often this is related to a person's race, but it might also be related to their religion or the country that they or their family come from.

government: the system that is set up to run a country. The word *government* can also refer to the people who are part of that system, like a mayor or lawmakers.

habitat: the place where people, animals, or plants live.

immigrant: a person who comes to live in a new country from a different country.

jury: a group of people who are asked to help make decisions in court, like whether a person is innocent or guilty of committing a crime. When a jury makes a decision, it is called a verdict.

justice: using laws and rules to treat people fairly and right. If justice is served, that means that people get the punishments or rewards that they deserve.

literacy: the ability to read and write.

persecute: to treat someone cruelly and unfairly, especially because of things like their race or religion.

pioneer: a person who goes new places or comes up with new ideas. In the 1800s, people who travelled west to settle new lands were referred to as pioneers. Today, the term is more often used to refer to someone who's helping to create something different or new.

politics: things people do to influence how a government works and who controls it.

pop culture: short for popular culture. That describes culture that appeals to a lot of people, like popular music or movies.

protest: When people protest, they express their unhappiness about something. The word *protest* can also be used to refer to a large gathering of people who have come together to demonstrate their unhappiness in a group, to draw attention to a cause.

ratify: to make something official by signing it or voting for it.

secede: to leave a country or group, often to become a new and independent one that controls its own affairs.

segregation: separating people who are different. Segregating people could mean separating people of different races, genders, or religions. In America, it usually refers to past attempts to separate black and white people.

slavery/slaves: a slave is a person who is owned by another person. Usually a slave is forced to work for their owner without payment or basic freedoms. *Slavery* is the practice of owning slaves.

territory: an area of land. If a country has a territory that means they own it or control it.

terrorism/terrorist: using violence or threats to scare people or achieve a goal. A terrorist is someone who uses these tactics, usually for political reasons.

treaty: an agreement made by people, groups, or countries. Often leaders of two or more countries will sign a treaty to make peace or achieve some goal, such as limiting nuclear arms or helping to stop global climate change.

tyranny: a government ruled by a person who treats people cruelly or unfairly.

war: a fight between groups or countries that often leads to the death of people in those groups or countries.

EXPLORE SOME MORE!

GOVERNMENT WEBSITES

Much of the information in this book was gathered from websites run by the government. The government's many departments gather data on everything from volcano eruptions to how much Americans weigh. You can learn more by visiting their sites and digging in on your own.

Centers for Disease Control and Prevention
Information on the health of people in America came from the Centers for Disease Control and Prevention—known as the CDC. Find out more about height, weight, and dangers to our health at **cdc.gov**.

U.S. Census Bureau
Information on the people who live in America came from the U.S. Census Bureau, which does a survey every ten years to see how many people live in the U.S. and what their households are like. You can learn more about things like race, income, and what languages Americans speak at **census.gov**.

U.S. Department of Agriculture
Agriculture is a word that describes the way people use land, grow crops, and raise animals. Information on things like imports, exports, and America's trading partners came from this agency. For more on this, visit **ers.usda.gov**.

U.S. Department of the Interior
The Department of the Interior is responsible for federal land and natural resources, as well as programs related to American Indians. Statistics about the land inside the U.S. and information about American Indians were collected from the Department's Bureau of Indian Affairs: **bia.gov**.

U.S. Department of State
Information like passport statistics and lists of useful American idioms came from the U.S. Department of State's website at **state.gov**. Go there to find out what the government is doing to keep peace around the world and help Americans travel safely.

U.S. Geological Survey
The USGS is a scientific agency that collects information about America's water and land, as well as the things buried in it and the things that might hurt it. You can find everything from volcano alerts to gold mine maps at **usgs.gov**.

Library of Congress
This is the largest library in the world! The library maintains archives and collections on American history and culture. You can check out the library's millions of books, recordings, and photographs at **loc.gov**.

National Archives and Records Administration
Information about the founding documents and other historical facts came from the National Archives. If you want to see a picture of the actual Constitution or Declaration of Independence, or read transcripts of these very important pieces of paper, go to **archives.gov**.

National Center for Education Statistics
Data about things like how many kids are graduating from high school and how many of America's kids know how to read came from the National Center for Education Statistics at **nces.ed.gov**.

National Institutes of Health
Information about medical research and medical history came from **nih.gov**. Head there to find facts about everything from America's weight problem to the dentist who invented cotton candy in the 1800s.

National Park Service
The National Park Service takes care of America's most famous landmarks. This book used oodles of information about landscapes and geography from **nps.gov**. You can find links to sites for all of America's national parks there. (Fourth graders can apply for a free national park pass, too!)

National Travel and Tourism Office
Data about who is visiting the United States—and where Americans are traveling—comes from **travel.trade.gov**. If you want to know where Americans' favorite travel spots around the world are, this is the place to go.

The U.S. Senate
Facts about how the government works came from the U.S. Senate's website, **senate.gov**.

The White House
Information about the white house's online petition program, the history of the building, and the presidency came from **whitehouse.gov**. Go there to learn about every single president that America has ever had.

State Governments
You can learn more about each of the 50 states by visiting the official sites of their governments. (Goodness knows the author of this book did!) Many of these sites have parts that are written just for kids. You can usually find them by searching in a web browser for "[Put the state name here] government for kids".

Alabama *alabama.gov*

Alaska *alaska.gov*

Arizona *az.gov*

Arkansas *arkansas.gov*

California *ca.gov*

Colorado *colorado.gov*

Connecticut *ct.gov*

Delaware *delaware.gov*

Florida *myflorida.com*
Hawaii *portal.ehawaii.gov*
Illinois *illinois.gov*
Iowa *iowa.gov*
Kentucky *Kentucky.gov*
Maine *maine.gov*
Massachusetts *mass.gov*
Minnesota *mn.gov*
Missouri *mo.gov*
Nebraska *www.nebraska.gov*
New Hampshire *nh.gov*
New Mexico *newmexico.gov*
North Carolina *nc.gov*
Ohio *ohio.gov*
Oregon *oregon.gov*
Rhode Island *ri.gov*
South Dakota *sd.gov*
Texas *texas.gov*
Vermont *vermont.gov*
Washington *access.wa.gov*
Wisconsin *wisconsin.gov*

Georgia *georgia.gov*
Idaho *idaho.gov*
Indiana *in.gov*
Kansas *kansas.gov*
Louisiana *louisiana.gov*
Maryland *maryland.gov*
Michigan *michigan.gov*
Mississippi *ms.gov*
Montana *mt.gov*
Nevada *nv.gov*
New Jersey *newjersey.gov*
New York *ny.gov*
North Dakota *nd.gov*
Oklahoma *ok.gov*
Pennsylvania *pa.gov*
South Carolina *sc.gov*
Tennessee *tn.gov*
Utah *utah.gov*
Virginia *virgina.gov*
West Virginia *wv.gov*
Wyoming *wyo.gov*

MUSEUMS AND OTHER ORGANIZATIONS

Museums are a great source of information on natural history, culture, and American history. The sites listed here were a great resource for information about the U.S.

Colonial Williamsburg Foundation

This foundation maintains an entire town from the British Colonial period and is dedicated to teaching and preserving American colonial history. Their website, *history.org*, is an excellent source for learning what it was like to live in America hundreds of years ago. Information about colonial times (including things like the clothes people wore back then) came from this organization.

The Field Museum

Chicago's Field Museum is where Sue the T. rex (or, at least, the dinosaur's famous fossils) lives. Information on this famous American dinosaur came from *fieldmuseum.org*.

Metropolitan Museum of Art

Famous art can tell us a lot about what it was like to live when that art was made. This book uses information on cultural history that came from the Met's website: *metmuseum.org*. Located in New York, this is one of the country's best art museums, and you can look at its 5,000 years worth of art online.

Mount Vernon

Mount Vernon was the name of George Washington's home. Information about colonial and revolutionary times came from its website, *mountvernon.org*. Go there for more on one of the Founding Fathers.

National Congress of American Indians

The National Congress of American Indians is the oldest and biggest organization dedicated to the tribes who have lived here for thousands of years. Information about the past and present of American Indians came from *ncai.org*.

The Smithsonian

There are 19 museums and galleries that are part of the Smithsonian, making it the biggest museum complex in the world. They hold everything from Dorothy's red ruby slippers to rooms full of live butterflies! This book used information about art, culture, sports, food, and history from the Smithsonian's websites. *si.edu* is a good place to start.

REFERENCE WORKS

The *Dictionary of American Regional English* was an invaluable resource regarding historical differences in speech across the U.S.

Hall, Joan Houston, ed., *Dictionary of American Regional English*, *Volume VI*. Cambridge: Belknap Press of Harvard University Press, 2012.

ARTICLES

Newspaper and magazine articles written at the time of historical events can tell you a lot about how people felt in times of yore, so can online articles written by historians who have had time to think about the impact of those events. The *New York Times* and *TIME Magazine* maintain online archives of their articles that were used in writing this book. Below are some examples of articles that were useful to the author:

From the *New York Times* archive (*timesmachine.nytimes.com*)
   "Dream Comes True in Lindbergh's Feat." The *New York Times*, May 22, 1927.

From the *TIME Magazine* archive (*time.com/vault*)
   "The Little Strike that Grew to La Causa." *TIME Magazine*, July 4, 1969.

INDEX

*Page numbers in bold (such as **142**) refer to images and maps.*

1700s life, 142, **142**
1800s life, 143, **143**
1900s life, 144, **144**
2000s life, 145, **145**

Adams, John, 12, **12**, 48, **48**
Adams, John Quincy, 48, **48**
Air Force One, 40, **40**
air travel, 98, **98**
Ali, Muhammad, 127, **127**
alligators, 185, **185**
American Dream, 139, **139**
American Indians, **8**, 8–9, **9**, 114–15, **114–15**
American Revolution, 14, **14**, **16**, 16–17, **17**
Angelou, Maya, 128, **128**
animals, **74–75**, 74–77, **76**, **77**
Armstrong, Louis, 130, **130**
atomic bomb, 101, **101**

Bell, Alexander Graham, 123, **123**
Bill of Rights, 24, **24–25**, 25
bills and laws, 29
bombing of Japan, 101, **101**
Boston Tea Party, 14, **14**
branches of government, **26–33**
Bush, George H. W., **44**, 45, **45**, 153, **153**
Bush, George W., 44, 45, **45**

capital, **62**, 62–63, **63**
cars, early, 99, **99**
Chavez, Cesar, 119, **119**, 133, **133**
citizens, 22
civil rights, 106–19
Civil Rights Movement, **106–7**, 112, **112**, 113
Cleveland, Grover, 49, **49**
Clinton, Bill, 44, 45, **45**
clothes, colonial, 15, **15**
colonies, original, 17, **17**
colonists, **10**, 10–11, **11**
Columbian Exchange, **164–65**, 165
Columbus, Christopher, **6–7**, 7
Common Sense (document), 18, **18**
communication technology, 104, **104**
Congress, 28, **28**
Constitution, 19, **19**, 22, **22–23**, 23
crocodiles, 185, **185**
crops, 165, **166**, 167, **167**

Declaration of Independence, 4, **4–5**, 19, **19**
Democrats, 35, **35**
deserts, 67, **67**
dinosaur skeleton, 182, **182**
Disney, Walt, 129, **129**
documents, important, 18, 18–19, **19**

eagles, bald, 183, **183**
Earhart, Amelia, 125, **125**
Edison, Thomas, 122, **122**
Einstein, Albert, 101
Eisenhower, Dwight D., 47, **47**, 153, **153**
elections, **34**, 34–35, **35**
Electoral College, 35, **35**
Ellis Island, 80, **80–81**
Emancipation Proclamation, 110, **110–11**
entertainment, **160**, 160–61, **161**
Everglades, 185, **185**
executive branch of government, 27, **27**, **30**, 30–31, **31**
explorers, **6–7**, 7
exports and imports, 158–59, **159**, **166**, 167

First Ladies, **42**, 42–43, **43**
Fitzgerald, Ella, 130, **130**
food and drinks, 174–75, **174–75**
Ford, Henry, 99, **99**
forests, 70, **70**

Founding Fathers, 4, **4–5**, **12**, 12–13, **13**
Franklin, Benjamin, 13, **13**
Freedom Tower, **188**, 188–89, **189**

Gershwin, George and Ira, 131, **131**
Gettysburg Address, 96, **96**
Gold Rush, 95, **95**
government, 20–37
Grand Canyon, 72, **72**
Great Lakes, 68, **68**
Great Plains, 71, **71**

Hamilton, Alexander, 13, **13**
happiness, **146**, 146–47, **147**
height, 141, **141**
House of Representatives, 28, **28**

idioms, 176–77
immigrants, 78–87
imports and exports, 158–59, **159**, **166**, 167
integration, school, 102, **102**
Internet, 104
inventions, American, **172**, 172–73, **173**

Jackson, Andrew, 46, **46**, 153, **153**
Jamestown, Virginia, 10, **11**
Japan, bombing of, 101, **101**
Jefferson, Thomas, 13, **13**, 46, **46**, 94
Johnson, Lyndon B., 49, **49**
Jordan, Michael, 127, **127**
Joyner-Kersee, Jackie, 127, **127**
judicial branch of government, 27, **27**, **32**, 33

Kennedy, John F., 49, **49**
King, Billie Jean, 127, **127**
King, Coretta Scott, 132, **132**
King, Martin Luther, Jr., **107**, 113, **113**, 132, **132**

language, **89**, 89–91, 155, 176–77
Latino rights, 118–19, **118–19**
laws, 29
legislative branch of government, 26, **26**, **28**, 28–29
life span, 140–41, **141**
Lin, Maya, 135, **135**
Lincoln, Abraham, 47, **47**, 96, **96**, 110, **110–11**
Lindbergh, Charles, 124, **124**
Little Rock Nine, 102, **102**
Louisiana Purchase, 94, **94**

Madison, James, 13, **13**, 48, **48**
Magna Carta, 18, **18**
March on Washington, 106, **106–7**, **112**, 113
Mayflower Compact, 18, **18**
McKinley, William, 49, **49**
Mid-Atlantic states, 53, **53**
Midwest, **54**, 54–55, **55**
military, 150–51, **151**
Mississippi River, 69, **69**
Model T cars, 99, **99**
money, **186**, 186–87, **187**
Monroe, James, 48, **48**
Montana, Joe, 127, **127**
moon landing, 11, **92–93**, 93, 103, **103**
Morse, Samuel, 123, **123**
mountains, 66, **66**
mountain states, **58**, 58–59, **59**
music, **170**, 170–71, **171**

New England, 52, **52**

Obama, Barack, **34**, **44**, 45, **45**
Obama, Michelle, **34**, 43, **43**
O'Keeffe, Georgia, 135, **135**
Old Faithful geyser, 184, **184**

Olympics, **156**, 156–57, **157**
One World Trade Center, **188**, 188–89, **189**

Pacific states, **60**, 60–61, **61**
Parks, Rosa, 133, **133**
Peace Corps, 154, **154**
petitions, 36–37
Pilgrims, 10, **10**, 11
political parties, 35
Polk, James K., 46, **46**
Pony Express, **178**, 178–79, **179**
population statistics
    United States, 88, **88–89**
    world, **148–49**
presidents
    birthplaces, 41, **41**
    election, 35, **35**
    eligibility requirements, 40
    life span, 141, **141**
    recent, **44**, 44–45, **45**
    stars, 48, 48–49, **49**
    superstars, 46, 46–47, **47**
    at war, 153, **153**

railroad, transcontinental, 97, **97**
Reagan, Ronald, 30, 49, **49**
Republicans, 35, **35**
Revere, Paul, 16, **16**
Robinson, Jackie, 126–27, **126–27**
Roosevelt, Franklin D., 47, **47**
Roosevelt, Theodore, 47, **47**, 153, **153**
Route 66, 179, **179**
Ruth, Babe, 126, **126**

seal
    presidential, 31, **31**
    United States, 183, **183**
Senate, 28, **28**
September 11, 2001 terrorist attacks, 105, **105**
settlers, **10**, 10–11, **11**
slavery, **108**, 108–11, **109**, 110–11
South, **56**, 56–57, **57**
sports, **168**, 168–69, **169**
states, 50–63
Statue of Liberty, 82–83, **82–83**
Sue (dinosaur skeleton), 182, **182**
Supreme Court, **32**, 33

T. Rex dinosaur skeleton, 182, **182**
Taft, William Howard, 49, **49**
timeline, 190–201
tourist spots, 180, **180–81**, 181
Treaty of Paris, 19, **19**
Truman, Harry S., 47, **47**
Tubman, Harriet, 109, **109**
turkeys, 183, **183**
Twain, Mark, 128, **128**

Underground Railroad, 109, **109**
United Nations, 155, **155**
U.S. Constitution, 19, **19**, 22, **22–23**, 23

volcanoes, 73, **73**

war, **152**, 152–53, **153**
Washington, D.C., **62**, 62–63, **63**
Washington, George, 12, **12**, 46, **46**, 153, **153**
weight, 141, **141**
White House, 31, **31**
White Sands National Monument, 185, **185**
Wilson, Woodrow, 47, **47**
women's rights, **116**, 116–17, **117**
World War I, 100, **100**
World War II, 101, **101**
Wright, Frank Lloyd, 134, **134**

Yellowstone National Park, 184, **184**